More from
THE TEXTILE
ARTIST series

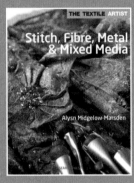

Stitch, Fibre, Metal & Mixed Media
978-1-84448-762-2

Appliqué Art
978-1-84448-868-1

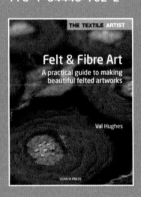

Felt & Fibre Art
978-1-84448-992-3

Layer, Paint and Stitch
978-1-78221-074-0

From Art to Stitch

DEDICATION

To Barbara Young.

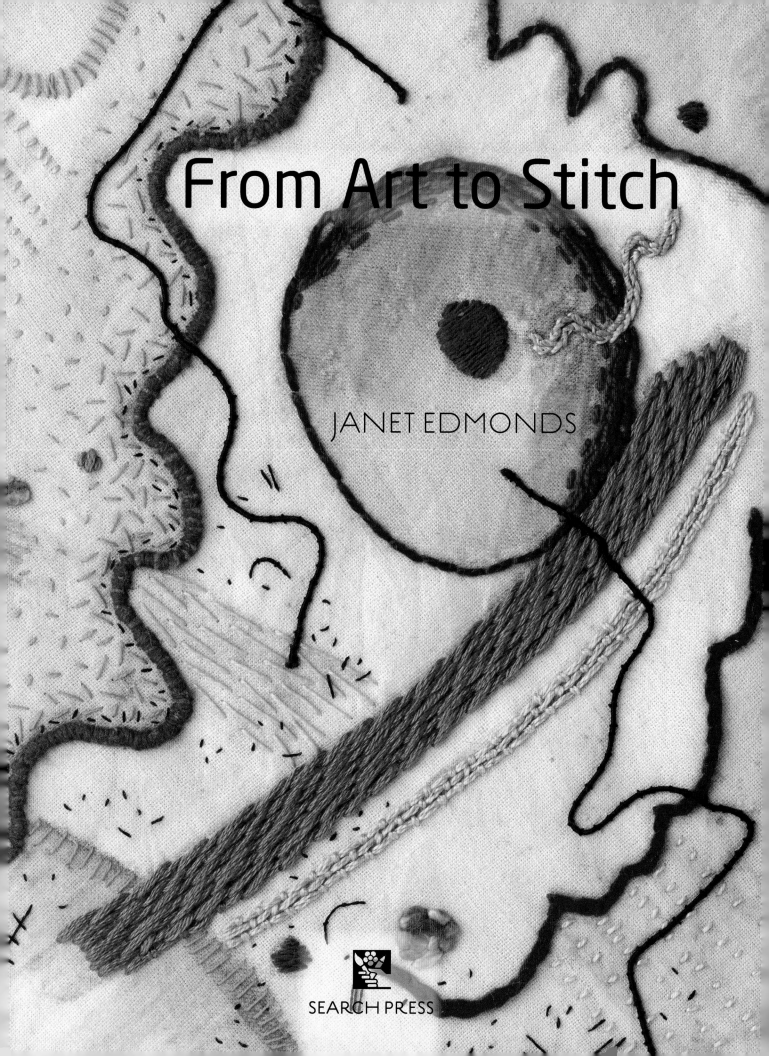

From Art to Stitch

JANET EDMONDS

SEARCH PRESS

First published in Great Britain 2015

Search Press Limited
Wellwood, North Farm Road,
Tunbridge Wells, Kent TN2 3DR

Illustrations and text copyright © Janet Edmonds, 2015

Photographs by Paul Bricknell at Search Press Studios

Photographs and design copyright © Search Press Ltd.
2015

ISBN: 978-1-78221-030-6

The Publishers and author can accept no responsibility
for any consequences arising from the information,
advice or instructions given in this publication.

Suppliers
If you have difficulty in obtaining any of the materials
and equipment mentioned in this book, then please visit
the Search Press website for details of suppliers:
www.searchpress.com

You are invited to visit the author's website:
janetedmonds.co.uk

Printed in China

ACKNOWLEDGEMENTS

My thanks go to Roz Dace for seeing the potential in
my idea for this book, Sophie Kersey for her support
and encouragement and the rest of the
Search Press team for bringing it to fruition.
I acknowledge, too, the support of my family for their
part in making it possible to write another book, and
also a huge thank you to all my students for their
continuing enthusiasm and interest in my endeavours.

Front cover

This Matisse-inspired wall hanging is also shown on page 142.

Page 1
Stitched Squares

This abstract panel was inspired by Chuck Close. Its development is
featured in that chapter and it also appears on page 35.

Page 2
Field of Wheat

Cotton and silk threads have been used for this sample of straight
stitching inspired by the landscapes of Van Gogh.

Page 3
Stitched Abstract

Stitching from a drawing inspired by the work of Kandinsky.

Above
Sample Book

This is the cover of the stitch sample book which is part of the
development of pieces inspired by Hundertwasser. The book is featured
on pages 84–87.

Opposite, left

This stitched sample shows textures from the work of Van Gogh.

Opposite, right
Wheat

This stitched piece was developed from a drawing I did inspired by a detail
from Van Gogh's 'Wheatfield with White Cloud,' 1889 (see page 39).

Contents

Introduction

The artists that I have chosen to explore for this book are those whose work I have admired for some time and keep returning to for inspiration. I have been interested in the art of the early 20th century, particularly in Europe, for a long time, and it is a rich, varied palette from which to choose. The first half of the century was a time of great freedom to experiment with all kinds of ideas and media, and has been referred to as 'a revolution in art'. In the latter part of the 19th century, artists began to question the old ways, testing the boundaries of acceptability. There was a break away from conventional painting to embrace more experimental approaches. The beginning of the 20th century saw artists continuing to push the boundaries. Public taste began to change and critics and gallery owners were more prepared to give credence to new ideas. Artists respond to the conditions of their time, and this period saw major events within Europe that affected the artistic work produced.

When looking for just a few of these artists to explore in more detail, I was spoilt for choice. I looked for design elements, themes and processes. I then applied the characteristics of each artist to my own images, to inspire original stitched work using a variety of approaches.

I begin with Chuck Close, a portrait painter. I am amazed by the accuracy of his depiction of the human face. Every blemish and hair follicle is painted with precision. Large paintings are divided into grids, with each square painted separately, but when viewed from a distance, they look like a photograph, even though each square, viewed in close up, is abstract. I show how working with a grid of squares can produce either accurate images or abstract pictures using one or a few squares. These are stitched using simple hand stitches.

Next I explore colour and surface texture through the work of Van Gogh. Many of his paintings are familiar, but closer examination reveals the texture of the paint, and the extraordinary colour compositions that are an inspiration for textured, stitched surfaces. On reading the letters that he wrote to his brother, Theo, I sensed that he experienced colour intensely, and that was what he was recording.

Hundertwasser, an architect, is the inspiration for my use of line. He designed buildings that grew out of the landscape and used bright primary colours in his map-like landscapes, with a linear style that meandered across the work. I am inspired by the quality of line and the strong vibrant colour in his work, and I combine these with appliqué and couching, resulting in designs for stitched boxes.

Kandinsky was one of the first artists to make purely abstract work that he based on notions of the mystical and musical. Although I like his paintings, I decided to work with his geometric shapes and eccentric structures. These are developed into small constructions made with found objects and electronic parts, incorporating stitching. My aim was to keep a playful aspect to the work and not to be concerned with achieving a practical outcome.

In contrast, Italian artist, Georgio Morandi, used quiet, close-toned colour to depict small still-life groups. His work lends itself to being combined with stumpwork-like stitching. I have kept to simple straight stitching with small dimensional vessels, stitched with buttonhole stitch or cast using various techniques.

John Piper's life spanned much of the 20th century, so his work moves through several styles. He was a war artist and experimented with print with his architectural drawings. I am always drawn to the printed mark, so wanted to reflect this and capture the scribbly style of his mark-making that works so well with buildings. I use machine stitch techniques with monoprint in this chapter.

Henri Matisse was another popular and prolific artist whose work developed through decorative simplification with light, colour and space. Much of his inspiration was drawn from textiles. I have used decorative digitally printed cloth, creating flat pattern combined with still-life subjects. Pattern is continued through the use of composite stitching, and piecing and patching.

Although I have spent some considerable time investigating these inspirational artists, there is still much to learn. There are many more artists who can inspire contemporary stitch and process. I hope you will be similarly inspired by these artists and perhaps research others that you admire. The history of the world's art is a rich seam of inspiration to tap into.

Looking for inspiration

Inspiration is all around us and we never have to look very far to find it. However, sometimes we may be stuck in a rut, looking at the same things in the same old way, and it may be helpful now and again to be a little more specific about what we are looking for.

It is always good to look at other artists' work, whether it is the work of other textile artists or the amazing, rich heritage of painting and the decorative arts that can be seen in museums around the world or in your own locality.

In this book, I have chosen some artists whose work inspires me. It may be work that I have seen in a gallery, a museum or a book but every time I see it, I am inspired and reinvigorated by it.

The artists I have chosen have very individual styles of work and each one offers scope for further investigation. I am not looking to emulate their work – that would not be possible or desirable – but I hope my practice will be enriched by observing how they have used colour and what kind of surface has been created. I can learn a lot by studying the composition and balance of imagery.

When viewing the work of great artists, it is helpful to consider the design elements and principles and observe how they have used them. I will refer to these later in the book as each artist is considered.

The featured artists have been chosen either for their subject matter or their processes.

'Chuck Close uses pixelated images and creates portraits in photorealism.'

'Matisse painted pattern and fabric in interior settings.'

'Morandi's paintings of still life objects are in a narrow neutral palette.'

'The work of Kandinsky is colourful and abstract, with floating shapes, symbols and line.'

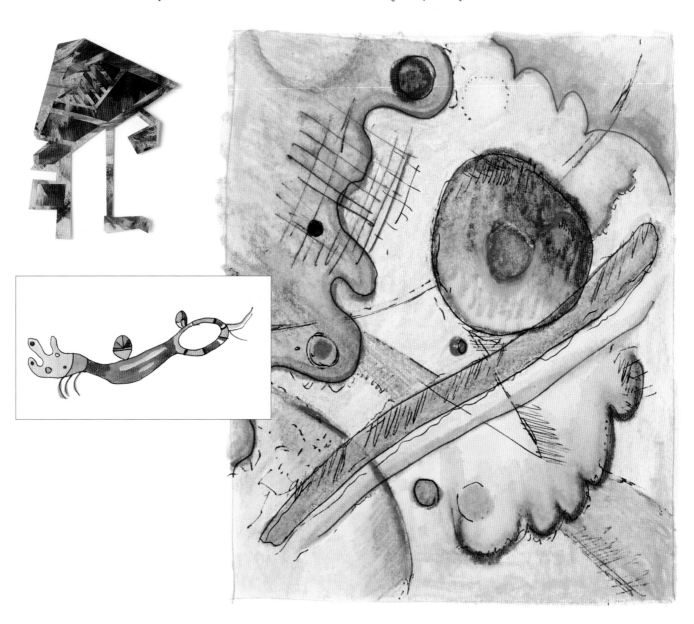

'I am drawn to the church architecture of John Piper and the way he combined colour with print.'

'Hundertwasser's work appeals to me with its eccentric form and linear qualities and riot of colour.'

'Van Gogh's paintings inspire with their exciting use of texture and wonderful colour combinations.'

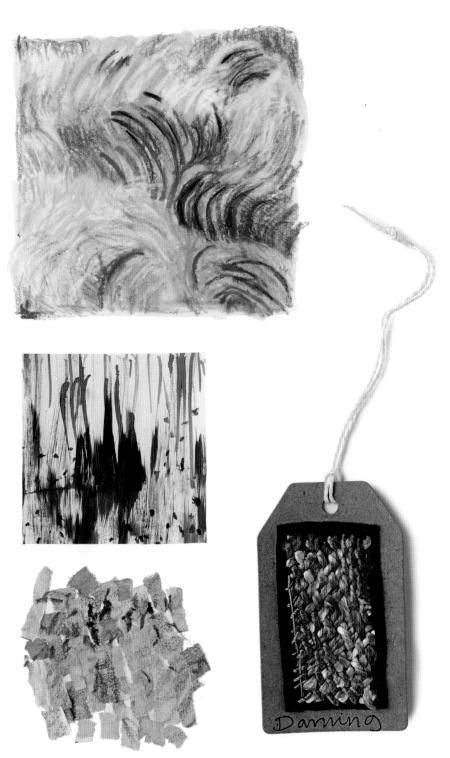

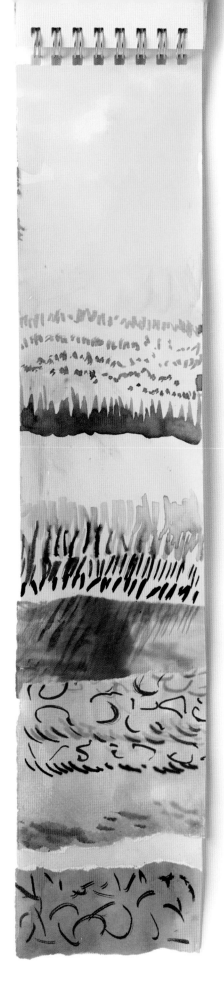

All in all, such a vast palette of inspiration cannot fail to excite and it was difficult to narrow down the material from such a rich and varied heritage of art.

I hope that this book will inspire the reader to discover the world's artists across a wide spectrum of disciplines, and that you will be stimulated to explore their work through stitching and textiles.

Materials

Giving consideration to what is needed to create drawings and designs is a difficult business as there are so many materials and items of equipment available for the contemporary textile artist, and the choice can be bewildering. Most of you will be well equipped already with a range of design materials, including some firm favourites, so for the benefit of the less experienced, I will include here the basic items that I use in my own work and in this book and have found useful. More specific items will be listed within the relevant chapters.

Drawing and design

Paper and sketchbooks

I like to record ideas inspired by primary sources and others in sketchbooks. I have several on the go at any one time and try to have a theme in place for each one to make it easier to reference work that I have done. It is useful to have different sizes of books too. I have a small one, usually A6, to keep in my handbag so that I always have somewhere to make notes or to scribble a quick drawing when I am on the go. A4 or square books about 20 x 20cm (8 x 8in) are not too daunting when starting a drawing and can be taken with me when I am out without being too cumbersome. I use A3 books and larger when I am back in the studio making more detailed work and exploring ideas. The one thing that characterises all my sketchbooks is the quality of the paper. I always want this to be tough enough to withstand any rough treatment that I might subject it to such as wetting, scratching, collage and application of glue without it tearing or buckling. But I want the surface to feel right too when I am making detailed drawings with a pencil or pen. As a general rule, the larger the sketchbook, the heavier the paper.

Individual sheets of cartridge paper are useful too when a single large drawing is being made and specific thicknesses or surfaces can be selected. Other types of paper that should be included in your collection are tissue, tracing and lightweight detail paper. If you are on a tight budget, waste papers can be recycled, such as brown wrapping paper or envelopes.

'Many a good idea has been recorded on the back of an old envelope.'

Tree Peony Rich daorites autumn moon 10.2012

Pens, pencils and crayons

I have a range of pens, from fine liners to reed pens and dip pens for use with inks. I like to have a choice so that I can make the appropriate marks for the task in hand.

I use drawing pencils ranging from 2B to 8B, graphite sticks and charcoal and like to combine these with inks, either in bottled form or powdered. Chalky pastels and Conté crayons are favourites too and are great for blending, smudging and smearing. Good quality coloured pencils are worth collecting. I have ordinary coloured pencils and water soluble crayons that I use on a regular basis.

Paints and brushes

Good brushes are expensive but a small selection ranging in size is invaluable. I use fine ones for drawing but also for intricate details when I am recording textures. For larger, bolder work, household brushes or foam brushes are suitable and more affordable.

Acrylic paints give good coverage on the paper, can be thinned down with water and are fixed when dry. This means that it is possible to add other media over the top such as washes of ink or dry media in the form of pencils or crayons.

You will need a palette or old plate to mix paint on, and a water pot. Kitchen paper is useful to mop up spills or blot off too much paint or ink.

'I treasure my good brushes.'

Additional materials for art and design

You might also need: paper scissors, a self-healing cutting mat, craft knife or scalpel and steel ruler. Useful adhesives include: PVA, archival paste, glue stick and contact glue. Mount board, grey board, foam board, waste card and corrugated card are useful for mounting and creating structures, and masking tape is always handy.

Fabrics

The fabric I use most often is calico, with cotton sheeting a close second. Natural fibres feel good, they dye easily and they come in lots of different weights and weaves. I colour my cotton fabrics with cold water dyes and include some thread too so that they work well together for stitching.

Silk fabrics are great to use when a different surface and handle are needed. Silk cotton mixes are good tempered and dye well too. I use acid dyes to colour these.

I usually back the fabric with either a non-woven fabric such as medium-weight interfacing, or muslin to give support to my stitching. I like the feel of a slightly firmer surface and it gives just enough thickness to make it easier to join and fasten off threads.

Threads

I have many favourites, mainly natural fibres such as cotton perle, crochet cotton, soft cotton, stranded cotton and silk twists. Rayon threads are tricky to use as they are slippery and springy, but worth the effort, as they bring a sheen to the work, contrasting with the matt types.

I like to dye my own threads to complement commercially coloured thread. I can achieve a variegated colour which is soft and gradual, and over time this is more economical. Pale colours can be over-dyed to adjust the tone or colour and break up the flatness of regular dyed thread. I look for creams, greys, pale blues, yellow or pinks as these can be darkened or brightened by over-dyeing.

'A collection of threads, with their enticing colour and wide range of qualities from matt to shiny, thick to thin, rough to smooth, creates an irresistible invitation to begin stitching.'

Additional materials

For construction:

Felt or craft-weight interfacing may be used to soften the surface of card before covering it with fabric.

For dyeing:

Dyeing materials and tools include cold-water or acid dye powders, salt, soda, urea, a bowl or bucket, measuring spoons and a larger spoon for stirring.

For sewing:

You will need a sewing machine and threads, a tufting foot, an embroidery hoop, a variety of hand-sewing needles and small scissors with accurate points for cutting and trimming thread, plus larger scissors for cutting out fabric. A stiletto is also useful for making holes.

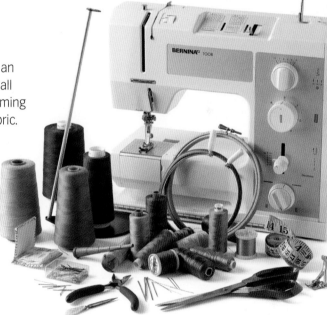

For printing:

You will need a sheet of acetate, plastic or glass with ground edges for rolling out paint; a roller, palette knife and printing inks, ideally water soluble. A piece of felt or thick foam is needed for cushioning the paper or fabric when making a print. This is especially important when using wooden print blocks. Paint extender is a useful product to add to acrylics if you are printing with them.

Chuck Close is an American, born 1940 in Washington. He is a painter, photographer and printmaker, and has pushed the boundaries of traditional printmaking, with some of his works taking more than a year to make.

Close creates large-scale, photorealistic portrait paintings and prints organised on a grid framework, which may be horizontal or diagonal. He uses strong, bright colour and also makes black and white tonal works. The marks he uses are brush strokes, fingerprints, dots, dashes, and paper pulp particles. Each square is painted individually, with brightly coloured, loosely painted shapes: circles, semicircles, targets, triangles and oblongs, doughnuts and teardrops. His colours are hot pinks, magenta, orange, cadmium reds and oranges, viridian, phthalo and emerald greens and cobalt, violet, ultramarine and cerulean blues. From a distance, the combined effect makes a realistic image.

None of Close's images are created digitally or photo-mechanically; they are all painstakingly made by hand. He is as concerned with process as he is with the resulting image. He says, 'My art is an invention of means rather than an invention of interesting shapes and interesting colours. It is a belief that ideas are generated by activity'.

His subjects are always people he knows, either family or friends, as he does not want to spend the time it takes to create a work with people he does not know. He has a condition called prosopagnosia, or face blindness, which means that he is unable to remember faces. Any small change, hardly noticeable under normal circumstances, makes recognition impossible for him. Perhaps this helps to explain why he works from photographs of well-known faces that capture a precise moment in time.

Close makes his portraits through a rigorous process of creating and editing a series of abstract marks that coalesce into a representational image. He does this by overlaying transparent colours, which are not skin colours, varying the order until he achieves the colour mix that he wants. He sees the face as a landscape, and describes his process as a scanning experience. The work is time-consuming, but his prints are more so.

A spinal infection in 1988 left him a paraplegic, but he continues to paint and make prints, daguerreotypes and tapestries.

Where to see his work

Close's work is in the collections of most of the great international museums of contemporary art, including the Centre Georges Pompidou in Paris, the Tate Modern in London, and the Walker Art Center in Minneapolis, USA.

'I make experiences for people to look at'.

Chuck Close

'I am always looking for how one piece can kick open the door for another possibility.'

Chuck Close

This is a coloured pencil drawing of a small section from one of Chuck Close's paintings. It shows the grid that is the underlying structure of his work and the way the image becomes abstract when seen square by square.

Reasons for choosing Chuck Close

The pixelated form is fascinating. I like the way an image can be divided up into sections, as it makes it possible to make much larger work, but in small bits, which is much less daunting than embarking on a large-scale work in one piece. Each square can be made individually and then several can be assembled to create a larger image. The squares may be joined or not, as wished. I am intrigued by each square of the coloured paintings of members of his family which are quite abstract and deceptively simple. They are, however, much more complex than they appear. Layers of colour are overlaid and constantly corrected until he is satisfied with the outcome.

The colour palette used by Chuck Close is bright and clear, which I am drawn to, but I am also inspired by his more neutral works. The two seem to complement each other and I find myself using two quite different colour schemes in the work that I do, one bright and bold and the other soft and neutral.

Looking at the grid process reminded me of a technique not much used now that employs a grid of squares drawn onto a picture or image to transfer or enlarge it onto another surface. A corresponding grid at a different scale is drawn onto a separate piece of paper. The image is then transferred, square by square, to recreate the picture at a different scale. The photocopier does this for us now. Having practised this technique, it is apparent that it is a very satisfactory way of getting to know the subject intimately, as every mark and nuance of colour is examined closely and then recorded as accurately as possible. Drawing people and portraits is a tricky business and achieving a likeness is very difficult indeed, but this method seems to overcome these difficulties if the time is taken to be methodical and accurate.

For this piece, I took a section from a Chuck Close silk screen print with a neutral colour palette, showing the eyes and spectacles of the subject. My version was made using acrylic paint.

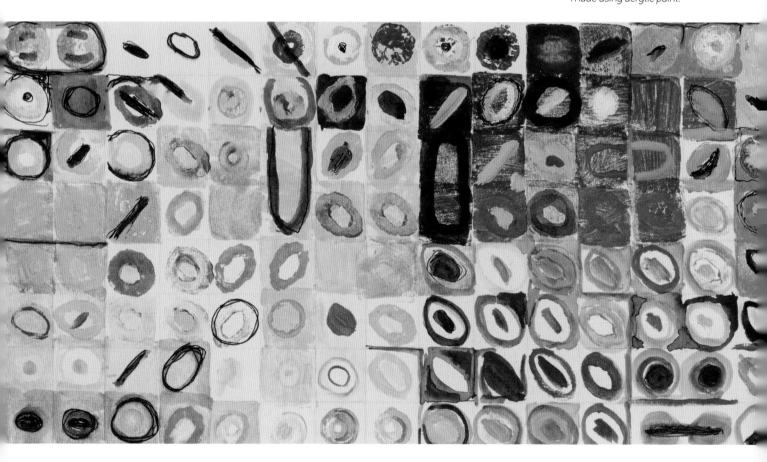

Working from the inspiration

I decided to develop two processes inspired by Chuck Close. The first is to use squares and fill them with colour to build an abstract image. Stitches will be used to cover the surface completely. This process could be developed for larger scale work, where scraps of fabric could be applied to a background and held down with decorative stitching.

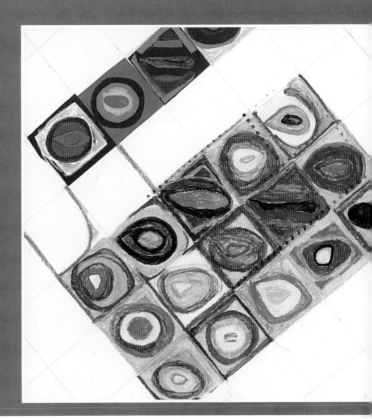

The second idea was to use a photograph of a member of my family and to transfer it to fabric using printed squares. Detail would be added onto the print with stitch to complete the portrait.

Both these strands of inspiration can be teased into other more complex areas of process to create a variety of imagery.

Scale

Working in small units makes it less daunting to create larger pieces of work, in much the same way as a whole quilt is built up from combining small unit blocks.

A design can be taken randomly from any picture or photograph, and it is then a simple process to change the scale. A 50mm (¼in) design could be reduced or enlarged just by changing the size of the square. This can be done manually or by using a photocopier or a design programme on computer. In practice, the larger the square, the more detail is required to give further interest on close inspection. Variation to the surface can be achieved with more elaborate texture or by adding dimension.

When stitching, detail may be added by either choosing more complex stitches to work the piece or by adding layers or texture. You can also scale up fabric and threads. Conversely, if the individual square is small, stitching should be done with fine thread and some detail left out. In the square pieces on page 37, I have used fine thread with simple straight stiches for the smallest square, and added fabric scraps and more textured stitching for the larger squares.

Another method of scaling up is to have more squares at the same size and either join them together, or place them onto a background fabric. Squares of different sizes could be placed together, either as a horizontal and vertical grid or as a diagonal grid by turning the squares on their points. I have given some more ideas using combinations of sizes of squares on page 27.

Working from one of Chuck Close's tonal images, a silk screen print, I selected a small section and began by recording the colours square by square. Next I printed the squares of the grid, first onto paper for the drawing and then onto fabric in preparation for stitching. I used a palette of blacks, white, greys and neutrals for this.

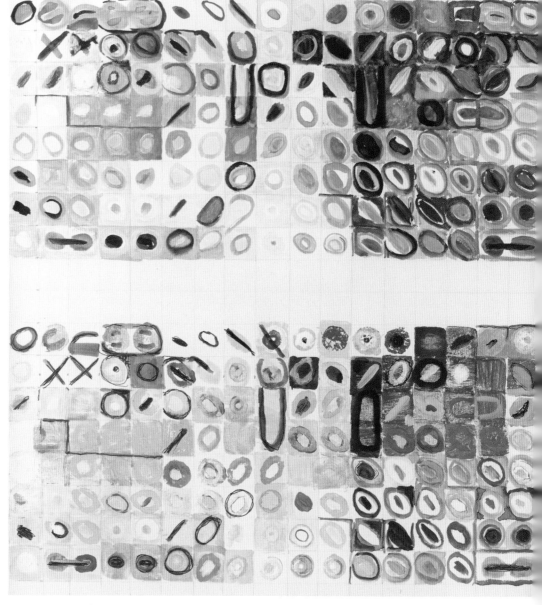

I was equally inspired by the portraits in colour and by the way that colour is built up in circular and oval form within each square. These images are Japanese woodcut prints and the one I tried out contains forty-three colours. I selected a small section from one of these prints, to record the randomness of laying the colours. I liked the effect, especially the way it was possible to take one square at a time. From my coloured drawing on page 21, I selected four squares and made a collage to simplify the colours (see left). I chose the squares randomly and eventually stitched twelve of them. I joined these together to get a larger image and used insertion stitches for this (see the finished piece on page 35).

It occurred to me that each small square at 5cm (2in) size would make a small brooch but would work at a larger size for a small panel or a cushion design (see page 37).

Using my own poppy photograph

I felt that there were more possibilities to explore from this inspirational artist. I did not want or intend to copy his imagery, indeed could not. Instead I took a photograph of a poppy in my garden and set about finding my own process.

Initially I made a colour drawing from the photograph, working square by square as described earlier, using coloured pencils on a good quality cartridge paper. Many embroiderers worry about drawing, but so much can be learnt from taking the time to do this stage and it is less daunting when one small square at a time is considered.

From this drawing I made a collage with paper that I had painted myself. Ready-made coloured papers could be used too. Making a collage helps to simplify the drawing because it makes it difficult if you have too many small, fiddly shapes to deal with. When cutting and sticking paper, you are obliged to reduce the detail. In addition, the collage makes a halfway stage between drawing and stitching.

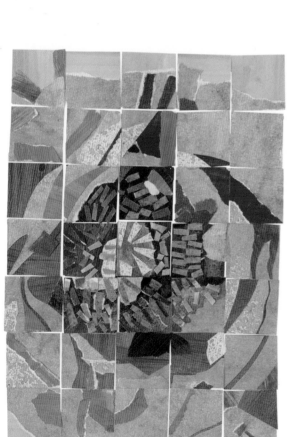

Working onto the poppy squares

I worked from the paper collage to make a sequence of printed squares. I had already simplified the image in the collage and I wanted to capture just the main areas of colour. When transferring into stitch, more detail can be added, and texture too, if that is required.

A decision needs to be made square by square, as to what the dominant colour is, and that is what I have printed. This works for most squares. Although there is variation within each square, one colour usually dominates. A few squares were divided half and half, with two contrasting colours. For these, I inked up the block with the two colours for printing. It is a good idea when doing this to make sure that the colours are the right way round, so check before printing.

The block for printing can be made in a variety of ways. Funky foam can be cut to size and stuck with strong glue to a piece of thick card. I use foam board for this as it gives a little more thickness for holding the block. Alternatively, a plastic eraser can be cut to size. This was the method I chose to use because I had an eraser that was exactly the size of the width and height of my squares. I used acrylic paint for printing, but fabric paint would be an alternative, especially if you are printing the paper and fabric at the same time. In this case, iron your fabric prior to stitching, to fix the colour.

When the paint is dry, finer details can be added to the paper print with coloured pencils. It is worth remembering that lighter colours can be made darker or brighter, but it is more difficult to put light colours over dark. If preferred, details can be added using acrylic paints.

Further experiments with the poppy squares

I have experimented with the design made from the poppy. There are many arrangements that can be made using the coloured squares randomly, as shown in the series of diagrams. Some squares could be joined together to make larger ones, or individual squares could be enlarged and combined with smaller ones. They will be easier to fit together in one design if they are in proportion to each other, for example, if the larger ones are twice the size of the smaller ones.

I enlarged the squares and made another collage. I added details using my drawing and the first collage as a reference, with some crayon drawing as a final stage. I colour photocopied this collage several times, enlarging and reducing so that I had several sizes to work with. Using the collage as a guide, I cut the squares out and arranged them on a contrasting sheet of green paper, without changing the order. I left a small gap between squares so that the contrasting green would show.

I made further arrangements, combining different sizes of square together and mixing up the order.

I also experimented with placing the coloured squares onto a network of a contrasting colour. I placed squares at the intersections of strips of paper.

Using a family photograph

I have repeated this process of working with squares with a photograph of my son, Tim, in keeping with the portraits that Chuck Close made of his family. I was not happy with the colour, so decided to work in a neutral palette using blacks, white and greys. I enlarged the photograph to twice the size and made a new drawing on the copy. I used a fine-liner pen to make stitch-like marks. Finally, I made another drawing, this time in colour, but first I printed the squares onto paper, taking the colours from the original photograph. At the same time, I printed the same colours onto fabric, ready for stitching. It may seem that there are a lot of stages before arriving at the point where stitching can begin. However, I find that if time is taken with preparation, the later stages are easier.

Opposite

A portrait of my son, Tim, following in the footsteps of Chuck Close, who made work from members of his family and close friends. The fabric was first printed with fabric paints using an eraser block. I then worked directional stitching over the top.

Stitch samples

I have used square designs taken from the squares in the collage on page 27 for most of these samples. This enables me to see the different effects of stitches and fabrics, and creates a valuable reference for future projects. I have sewn the samples into a concertina book for convenience.

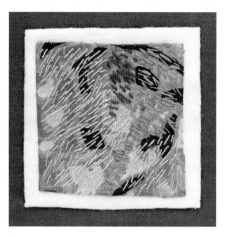

Satin stitch

I used stranded cotton on cotton fabric, with two strands of thread in the needle, to make long stitches, quite close together. This is the maximum length possible with this thickness of thread. Any longer and the stitches will stretch and loop and will not lie flat on the fabric. I couched a variegated rayon machine thread onto the background area. This is a variation of Bokhara couching, commonly worked as a filling stitch, where the same thread is used for the laid thread and the holding thread. I left spaces in between the diagonal rows so that the coloured background fabric shows through. The fine thread provides a contrast to the heavier satin-stitched areas. Rayon thread is tricky to use, as it is slippery, but its glossy surface is worth the struggle, providing contrast to the matt threads.

Directional straight stitch

This is one of the most useful methods of stitching and one that I have used most frequently, as it can give a painterly effect. Cotton threads were used throughout, with the addition of rayon for a contrast of scale. The background is a commercially printed cotton fabric, showing through the spaced stitches.

Straight stitches

These are organised into a pixelated grid form. The grid is shown by laying black cotton threads across the space and fixing them where they cross with a tiny stitch. Straight stitches are worked into the small squares.

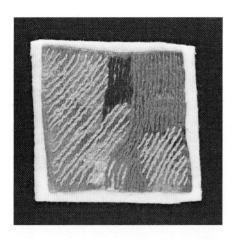

Split stitch

Lines of split stitch are laid close together as filling stitches, in varying directions.

Straight stitch

Small stitches are worked over painted canvas. Care needs to be taken to prevent a loosely woven fabric such as canvas from distorting during stitching. When stitches are worked in the same diagonal direction, the tension is liable to pull the fabric out of shape. I have changed the direction to keep the fabric lying flat.

Insertion stitches

These stitches are used to join edges of fabric together and were traditionally used on domestic items such as sheets and pillowcases as well as garments. The technique is sometimes known as 'faggoting'. In the context of experimentation, they may serve as decorative joinings for stitched tiles and squares. The two edges to be joined should be supported by tacking them to a piece of paper, a glazed cotton fabric or another firm, smooth fabric. This ensures that the distance between the two edges is even.

Shown here are, from left to right: bullion bars, faggot bundles and knotted insertion. There are other variations that can be found in any good stitch book. The work is removed from the supporting paper or fabric when stitching is complete, by snipping the tacking stitches at the back.

Sample book

This concertina book is a convenient way to package a collection of stitch samples for reference. It is small, easily stored and very portable. It is made with a plain, dark green fabric as background to the colourful samples. The contrast shows the stitching to good advantage. Each sample is worked onto a background fabric that is hemmed to a piece of white cotton fabric to give a border. This in turn is hemmed to the dark green base fabric. The strip is stiffened with craft–weight interfacing and the concertina is held together with a hand–twisted cord constructed from three different threads.

Stitched Squares

The finished project, the culmination of my processes inspired by Chuck Close. My original drawing of coloured squares inspired this small panel. Individual squares were worked using small straight stitches and then stretched over card. They are backed with silk and joined together with bullion bars.

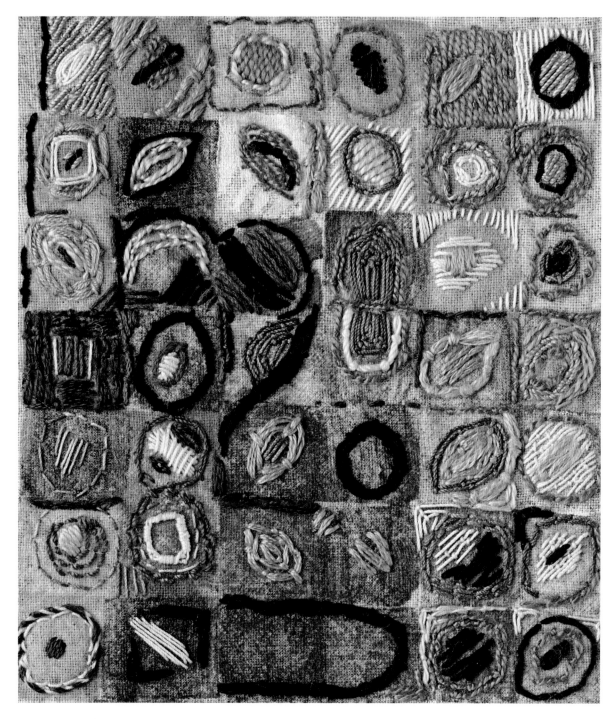

Stitching worked from the tonal drawings I made from Chuck Close's silk screen image. The fabric was first printed using a small square of wood and fabric paint, with the stitching worked over the top. Stitches include straight, chain, backstitch and couching, all worked with cotton threads.

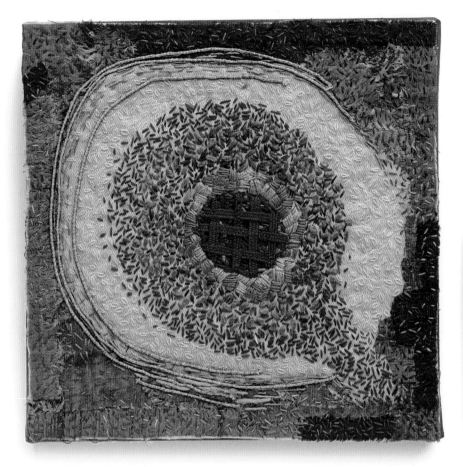

The original coloured pencil design.

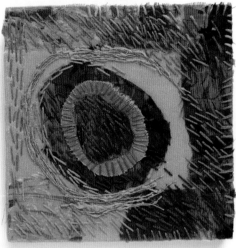

For this piece, which is 20cm (8in) square, I used scraps of coloured fabric as a border and worked small straight stitches over the top, blending colours together. I applied a larger piece of yellow fabric for the central area and worked detached chain stitches with a matching colour over the top, to add texture without changing the colour. The centre area has a grid of needleweaving as a focal point within the composition, surrounded by closely packed satin stitch and seeding in a variety of thread thicknesses. Couched gimp cord adds a contrast in colour and texture.

This piece is 10cm (4in) square. Yellow fabric provides the background, with scraps of printed silk fabric applied over the top. I added straight stitches and couching for texture and interest.

One small square makes an ideal design for a brooch; this one is 5cm (2in) square. It is worked on a canvas background with straight stitches completely covering the surface. It is backed with thin card covered with a matching fabric. I fastened a pin to the back before I stitched the front and back together.

A design for a brooch with nine small squares stitched in the centres with cotton perle thread in fly stitch and sorbello stitch. It is edged with a fine cord and small straight stitches.

There is much written about this popular artist, so I will be brief in my précis of his life. Vincent Van Gogh (1853–1890) was born in Holland. His father was a clergyman and his mother had a gift for watercolours. He spent time in France, Belgium and England as well as Holland, and much of the detail of his life is documented in the letters he wrote to his younger brother, Theo, to whom he was very close. They had a pact always to support each other and to write to each other on a regular basis. As a result, we have an insight into the thoughts and desires of the artist, as he described his work and the problems he encountered in the many letters to Theo.

After a failed relationship, Van Gogh developed an obsession with religion. He found that drawing was a therapeutic activity that helped to keep his depressive tendencies at bay. He had studied theology, but his eccentric habits led to his rejection by the church, so he turned to art.

Van Gogh was friends with the artists, Henri de Toulouse-Lautrec and Paul Gauguin, and his main artistic influences were Eugène Delacroix and Adolphe Monticelli. Delacroix said that: 'First and foremost, a painting should be a feast for the eyes'. In response to this, Van Gogh developed a distinctive style, using short, hatched, rhythmic marks with thick paint. This was an expressive, modified form of pointillism, with dots and dashes painted directly from nature. He painted still life subjects, landscapes and portraits of ordinary people he met.

Van Gogh's friendship with Gauguin was strained, and eventually broke down. It was at this time that Van Gogh cut off his ear with a razor. There is much controversy about the actual facts surrounding this event. He spent time in a mental institution, suffering from depression, misuse of alcohol and syphilitic infection. He went voluntarily and while there, did some of his best painting. There were times when he painted compulsively.

His life ended tragically at the age of 37. He is believed to have shot himself, but this too is shrouded in mystery and speculation. He had achieved in less than ten years a huge body of work that was virtually unknown when he was alive.

Few of Van Gogh's paintings were sold during his lifetime, but this changed after the first major exhibition of his work in Paris in 1901. This prestigious exhibition put him at the heart of the art scene, where young artists of the day such as Picasso, Matisse and Derain were given, in the words of Gauguin, 'the right to dare anything'. The expressive originality of Van Gogh's work was influential in the formation of Expressionist groups in Europe such as *Die Brucke* and the *Fauves*. Van Gogh's paintings must be some of the most well known, with his sunflowers and empty chair images instantly recognisable. He has a very distinctive style, with a spontaneous quality to the brush strokes. Blocks of colour, directional marks, long and short, staccato dabs of colour and bands of texture are all typical of his work.

Van Gogh liked to paint everyday objects, familiar places and ordinary working people he knew. The paintings and drawings were usually done from life, or from memory, but he was trying to paint not only what he could see but also what he felt about it. He felt that painters should paint things as 'they themselves feel them to be'.

He wished to make art that would depict the extraordinary nature of ordinary people, objects and places. His work shows energy, originality, movement, and the dignity of people going about their mundane lives.

Van Gogh firmly believed that painting should be accessible to everyone and that it should change people's lives for the better. He has become a legend and is an inspiration for many.

'Van Gogh wanted to recreate the human condition and this was what drove his art; the textures and colours conveying a sense of the unending struggle of day-to-day life.'

Where to see the work

Museums all over the world hold paintings, drawings, letter sketches and graphic works by Van Gogh within their collections, so I mention just a few. The Van Gogh Museum, Amsterdam holds the largest collection. The National Gallery, London, has some well-known paintings. The Pushkin Museum, Moscow, holds 'The Red Vineyard'; the only picture sold during Van Gogh's lifetime. The Kroller-Miller Museum in the Netherlands has 'The Café Terrace on the Place du Forum' and 'Arles at Night'. The Museum of Modern Art, New York holds 'The Starry Night'.

This is my version of a detail from one of many paintings of a sower that Van Gogh made towards the end of his life, when he found inspiration in painting the seasons. He believed that the sower represented the beginning of the cycle of life. The original, 'The Sower', was painted in 1888.

I took this detail from 'Wheatfield with White Cloud' 1889. Both details show the energetic brush strokes that provide great inspiration for stitched marks.

Reasons for choosing Van Gogh

Van Gogh's paintings have inspired and captivated countless people from all walks of life. Many of his works are so familiar that it is difficult to see them with fresh eyes. As an embroiderer, the appeal for me is two-fold: the colour and the texture. I love the colour relationships, the vibrant mixes of colour and the way the paint appears on the surface, giving depth and physicality to the subject. There is a spontaneous energy to the marks, expressing not only what is seen but also what is felt. The marks: blocks of colour, directional long and short brush strokes, staccato dabs of colour and bands of texture, are all suggestive of stitch marks, inviting exploration with fabric and thread.

I also like the fact that his work illustrates what was immediately around him. The interiors, objects, landscapes and portraits of himself and his friends; ordinary things, places and people, demonstrate that it is not necessary to go far for inspiration.

Here in my sketchbook, I have recorded some of the colour combinations seen in Van Gogh's work; the emotionally charged use of complementary colours: blue and orange, red and green, and yellow and purple , and the energetic marks, directional movement and vibrant brush strokes .

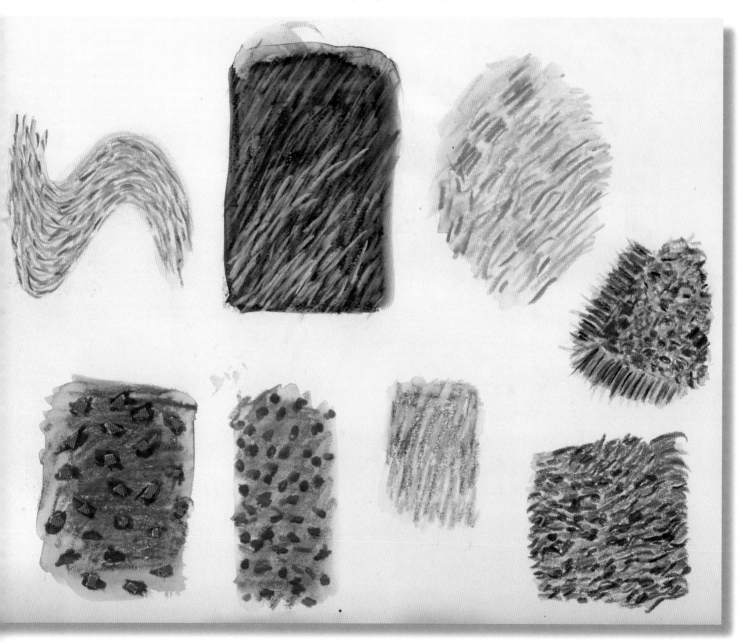

'We have only to see what is before us to be inspired.'

Working from the inspiration

'Ah, these farmhouse gardens with the lovely big red Provence roses, the vines, the fig trees; it's quite poetic...'

Vincent Van Gogh

Van Gogh, quoted above from one of his letters, was clearly inspired by the gardens he saw. His painting has inspired both colour and texture in the work of other artists. I have explored colour relationships and textures both actual and implied. Actual texture is raised and has physical depth, whereas implied texture is drawn or painted in such a way as to make it appear raised.

Where possible, I give references for particular paintings so that readers may look for themselves and experience the richness of colour and mark.

There is such a wealth of colours to choose from that making a selection is bewildering, so I have tried to limit the investigation to colour groups such as: red, green and orange; green, turquoise and blues; yellows and purples; neutrals and pale colours. Beyond these categories, there is still much to explore and to be inspired by. I began by extracting the colour mixes from specific paintings and recording these. Some of these were drawn, so they are smooth and flat, but I hope that they suggest depth. Once combinations had been identified, I worked with these to make texture marks that may suggest stitches or manipulated fabric surfaces.

The way that Van Gogh placed the colour describes movement and direction, and I have tried to capture this with my experiments at the design stage, but also with fabric and thread.

Collage is a useful technique, as the surface can be manipulated and raised by building up layers of coloured paper. The coloured papers can be crumpled, folded, torn and distressed. I have used some torn papers with drawing over the top, and placed some to create curves or spirals. Cut or torn paper can be rolled into beads and I have used this method to add texture to the collage. Working with coloured papers, I have incised and cut into them and then layered them one on top of another to create physical depth, shadows and spaces. Each layer is pasted so that it lies with folds and curves, making it possible to see the colours below.

I have pasted together two different coloured papers. I tore these into small pieces, folded them and stuck them to a background. The resulting texture gives colour on both sides of the paper.

I have used water soluble crayons, pens and brushes with inks, and placed the marks in rows or randomly to blend the colours. Scribble texture can be created with these tools and directional marks can be made too. A reed pen will give the kind of marks that we can see in Van Gogh's drawings because that is the tool he used.

Using colour

In his frequent letters to his brother, Theo, Van Gogh often described the colours that he saw. Reading these descriptions creates a vivid mental picture of the landscape or object he was writing about.

We are used to being faced with a sheet of white paper to which we apply colour, and often we only think about dark on light. I am inspired by the way Van Gogh layered pale yellows over deep purples and browns, and by his combinations of reds with yellows, and acid yellow with blue. He managed to create a sense of heat or cold in the way he combined colour.

'...a light that, for want of a better word, I shall call yellow, pale sulphur yellow, pale golden citron. How lovely yellow is'.

Vincent Van Gogh

'Under the blue sky, the orange, yellow, red patches of flowers take on an amazing brilliance and in the limpid air, there's something happier and more suggestive of love than in the north.'

Vincent Van Gogh

The inspiration I have drawn from Van Gogh's work in the form of colour and texture has been recorded on these strips (below and opposite) using the kind of marks seen in the paintings. Dots and diagonal dashes, flecks and mixes of colour and tone are shown. I used cut and torn paper and paint and ink applied with a brush and pen. Some of the strips have been developed into stitch samples, shown on pages 49–51.

Van Gogh used a vast array of blues and greens, creating a sense of the weather or of his mood on a particular day. The energetic, vigorous marks suggest the very experience he was witnessing. Warm blue, cold turquoise, mixed with acid yellow and orange, dark greens and pinks, all describe feelings of place and circumstance. He also used pastels and other interesting mixes to convey subject and mood. Looking closely into these paintings and observing how they are made inspires a bolder use of colour and a more dynamic method of applying it.

'The Mediterranean has the colours of mackerel, you don't always know if it is green or violet, you can't even say it's blue, because the next moment the changing light has taken on a tinge of pink and grey.'

Vincent Van Gogh

'Perhaps now I'll have a try at doing greens. Now autumn – that gives you the whole range of tones.'

Vincent Van Gogh

'I have made a series of colour studies in painting simply flowers...seeking oppositions of blue with orange, red and green, yellow and violet, seeking the broken and neutral tones to harmonise brutal extremes.'

Vincent Van Gogh

  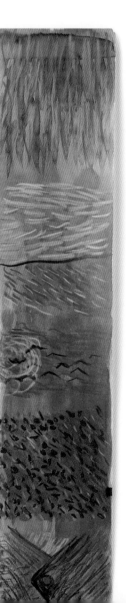 

Before doing the work for this chapter, I assumed that Van Gogh's colour palette was bright and vibrant. It certainly is, but he also used pastels and other mixes subtly and effectively. He included tiny amounts of complementary colours with dots, dashes and flecks to enliven the surface; all good devices to try out with our own work.

It is a good idea to experiment with paints and crayons to fully understand how to mix particular colours. There are a number of good books available that explain the theory of colour and how pigments work, but it is helpful to know your own materials, how to use them and what effects you can get with them.

With each primary colour, I have used several different pigments, as combining more than one type of red, yellow or blue will give a richer mix of colour. For instance, for yellow, I have chosen a lemon yellow and combined it with cadmium yellow. When each of these is mixed with red, oranges can be achieved, but the colour will depend on which red is used with which yellow. Alizarin or carmine red has a blue bias, whereas cadmium red is more orange. Similarly, when yellows are mixed with blue, there is a warm purply blue such as ultramarine, or a cool, greeny blue, often called phthalo or cerulean blue.

Each blue will make a different type of green when mixed with yellow. When using paints, confusion may arise over the names, as there does not seem to be a standard set, and different manufacturers may use alternatives. By using your own paints and crayons, you will come to know, with practice, which to choose to mix the colour you want.

'I love Van Gogh's neutral mixes of soft greens, delicate pinks, blues and greys.'

Here are further experiments with paint and paper, made with a variety of tools, to explore combinations. Techniques include dragging, flicking, wet in wet, dry on dry, tearing and piecing. All serve to inspire stitching.

Creating texture

Choosing a background for stitching

The choice of background is important, firstly to make the stitching a pleasure to do and secondly to ensure an integrated finished effect. I use a variety of methods. If I am using a plain fabric, I dye it to blend in with the planned stitching. I also back it with a fine, loosely woven fabric such as muslin, fine cotton or calico to support it while I work. I may texture the fabric with some free machining before I work hand stitches on it, or I may add fabric shapes if that is applicable to the end result.

A further method is what I call 'minced fabric'. This involves making a fabric with a mixture of tiny scraps of offcuts and thread. These can be placed onto a dissolvable support for stitching or onto a suitable piece of fabric. Either method requires the scraps to be placed in an embroidery frame for support while free machining is worked to blend the bits together. A matching or contrasting coloured thread can be used – the choice will depend on what is required in the finished piece of fabric. The resulting fabric makes a great background for further stitching by hand or machine.

I find it useful to have a ready supply of fabric scraps available for making my own surfaces, so I save any trimmings of fabric and thread from other projects and store them in colour-coded bags until they are needed. It may sound overly frugal, but it is a chore to have to cut up fabrics and threads to make this type of surface. It also ensures that there is a variety of colours and tones available for any new project.

Manipulated fabric

Working from the paper manipulation samples at the bottom of page 41, I have layered up fabrics that have first been machine stitched and then slashed. The fabrics I have used are rayon and chiffon and I have chosen the colours to include some contrast so that when the layers are fixed, one on top of another, the lower colours will show through.

I have also experimented with another method of layering two fabrics. The top one is loosely woven and the lower one is fine chiffon or silk. The chiffon is pulled through the gaps between the threads of the open-weave fabric on top (top right). It is not an easy technique to master but it is worth it. It is easier to work if the top fabric is under tension in a frame. Pull the threads apart and use a needle to catch a bit of the lower fabric and pull it to the surface. Anchor it in place with a small cross stitch and then move to the next gap between the top fabric threads and continue. I have used this method for the little round bag (below left), also shown on page 54. The reverse side of the fabric is neatened and lined with the small cross stitches used to hold the chiffon in place. The surface is finished with a layer of tiny beads set into the manipulated fabric, with the top edge gathered onto an expanding metal frame.

Fringing

Fringing may be made on a metal frame. The thread is wound round the frame until enough thickness is achieved, and then the ends are tied to the plastic stretchers. A line of machine stitching is made through the centre of the wound thread. This may be worked with either a straight line or a zigzag stitch, making sure that all the threads are caught down. The fringe is finished by sliding it off one end of the frame, folding it in half and running a machine stitch line down the stitched edge. Finally, snip the loops of thread with sharp scissors. This type of frame will enable wider fringing to be made by placing the metal runners into alternative holes in the stretchers.

Fringing frame showing wound thread.

Textured stitching

There are many stitches that can be used for texture. This sample is created with buttonhole bars. The bars are placed to stand proud of the fabric surface and massed closely together. I used a hand-dyed variegated cotton thread and worked another fine layer over the first using a machine thread in a contrasting colour. I wanted the effect to look as if a fine dusting of colour had been brushed across the stitching. Further stitch samples are shown below.

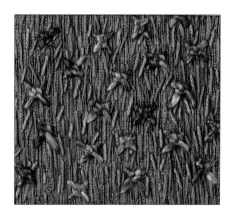

Sorbello over straight stitches.

Seeding stitches in red and blue.

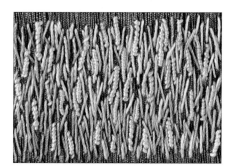

Straight stitches massed together in one direction. Some are whipped with a thicker thread to add dimension.

Beading

Many of the fabric and stitch textures inspired by Van Gogh's work lend themselves to interpretation into beaded surfaces.

Top row: wrapped fabric background is the support for bugle beads placed on their ends with tiny round beads to hold them in place. This is an effective surface when the beads are massed together.

Bugle beads are set with small squares of painted plastic onto a stitched background.

Cable stitching on the machine is the background to strings of yellow beads, laid in curves to complement the stitching.

The background fabric was textured with free machine stitching, then I added small massed beads on top. I added a machine-made fringed edge as described opposite.

47

Stitch samples

There are many hand-worked stitches to choose from, but for my own work I use mainly straight stitches, as they are so versatile. They link to corresponding marks made with a pen or pencil when I am drawing. They can be closely spaced or placed wide apart or in drifts. They can be worked in rows, horizontally or vertically, in groups or singly. They can be long or short, straight or slanting and the look of them can be varied according to the thickness and quality of the thead (whether matt, shiny, twisted tightly or loosely) and the tension of the working. Straight stitches are great for blending colour or layering for texture and they are simple to work.

Variations of straight stitch giving a different kind of mark include running stitch, backstitch, cross stitch, satin stitch, seeding and darning.

Alternatively, if texture is required, Cretan, buttonhole and wrapping are good choices of stitch, and these also can be layered to blend colour.

Stitching by machine widens the palette significantly but I have kept my experiments in the context of Van Gogh's work mainly to hand methods, with occasional use of the sewing machine where necessary.

Here are two brooches demonstrating the use of straight stitches. They show how colour can be enriched by blending several tones together and working further stitches on top.

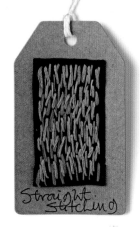

These small samples show the variety that can be achieved using the family of straight stitches.

Stitched studies in colour and texture

I have made a series of colour studies using stitch to express mood and texture observed in Van Gogh's paintings. I used both hand and machine stitching. Below and over the page, I list the techniques and materials I have used for each sample and the paintings that I have referenced.

Blues

The paintings that I have looked at for this sample are: 'Self Portrait with Bandaged Ear', 1889; 'Portrait of Dr Gachet', 1890; 'Portrait of Vincent Van Gogh, the Artist's Grandfather', 1881; 'Self Portrait', Spring 1888; 'Self Portrait in Front of Easel', 1888.

Many of Van Gogh's portraits use a variety of blues. Some are mixed with greens and turquoise; others show light blue on dark or dark on light. I have interpreted these textures and colours with these methods:

Red on Blue

Paintings used: 'Young Peasant Woman with Straw Hat, Sitting in the Wheat', June 1890; and 'La Mousme, Sitting,' July 1888.

Van Gogh often painted red dots on blue garments. I have explored different ways of using these colours together.

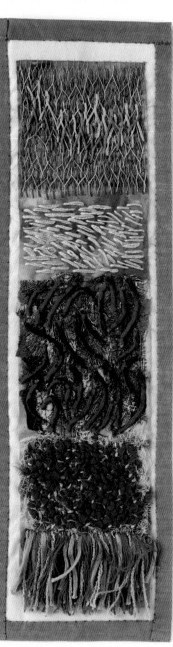

1 Cretan stitch in blues and greens and several thicknesses.

2 Light blue straight, directional stitches on a dark background.

3 Short lengths of rat-tail cord couched onto 'minced fabric' constructed by machine.

4 A manipulated surface made by pushing fine chiffon through an open-weave scrim with added seeding stitches and French knots.

5 Fringing made as described on page 46.

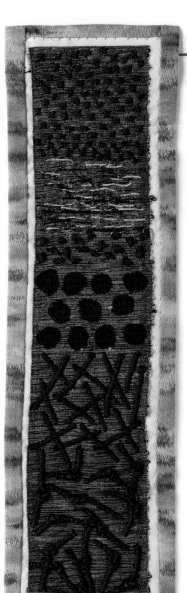

1 Sorbello stitches placed close together.

2 Machine satin stitch beads, leaving the connecting thread in place.

3 Red and blue thread blended with machine straight stitch.

4 Machined spots with a hand-tied knot on top.

5 Circles of fabric with free machining to hold them in place.

6 Rat-tail cord machined in place.

7 Rat-tail cord with blue zigzag on top, cut into lengths, a knot tied in the centre of each and hand couched.

Yellow hand stitch

Paintings used: 'Wheat Field with Crows', July 1890;
'Wheat Field with a Lark', 1887; Blossoming Almond Branch in a Glass',
1888; 'The Sower', October 1888; 'Willows at Sunset', Autumn 1888;
'Wheat Field with Sheaves', June 1888.

Yellows feature in abundance in Van Gogh's work: lemon yellows, warm cadmium yellows and deep orangey yellows, and they are combined with rich oranges and reds, purple hues and rusty browns. They light up the work, which might be surprising when the artist was such a depressive. I have explored arrangements of straight stitches using u variety of yellows and purples.

Yellow textures

Paintings used: 'Wheat Field with Crows', July 1890;
'Blossoming Almond Branch in a Glass', 1888; 'The Sower', October 1888;
'Willows at Sunset', Autumn 1888; 'Wheat Field with Sheaves', June 1888;
'Vincent's House in Arles (The Yellow House)', 1888.

This sample explores textured surfaces inspired by the way the paint is applied to the surface of the paintings.

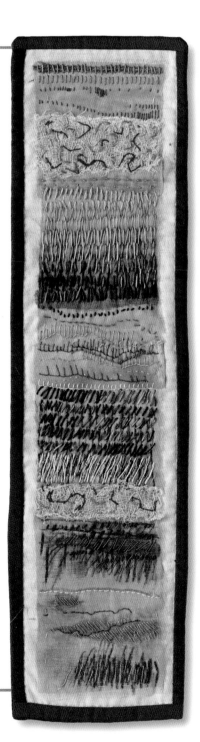

1 Spacing of straight stitches.

2 Short lengths of couching.

3 Rows of straight stitches ranging from pale yellow through to deep purple.

4 Buttonhole stitch.

5 Sloping straight stitches.

6 Straight lines of couching, blending colours.

7 Directional straight stitches. Long stitches worked with a fine thread will need a holding stitch to prevent them being baggy.

1 Small felt pieces applied in a random arrangement.

2 Small pieces of velvet fabric applied in rows.

3 Handmade felt cut into narrow lengths and couched.

4 Thick woollen rug yarn is couched and used as padding for the shiny rayon thread stitched over the top .

5 Tiny curved tucks are stitched with red thread and the fabric stitched down with straight stitches.

6 Dyed cotton fabric is textured by machine before being tucked.

7 Straight stitches have been wrapped with cotton thread and (below) mixed with directional straight stitches.

Greens and turquoise

Paintings used: 'Self Portrait with Bandaged Ear', 1889;
'Portrait of Dr Gachet', 1890; 'Wheat Field with Crows', July 1890;
'Fritillaries', 1887; 'Trees in the Garden of Saint-Paul Hospital', 1889;
'Self Portrait', 1889.

Many of Van Gogh's paintings have a wonderful textural surface. The paint is applied thickly, with raised directional gestures, and it is these that have inspired a range of surfaces using fabrics. I wanted to experiment with the sense of movement that so many of his paintings convey.

Neutrals

Paintings used: 'Orchard in Blossom (Plum Trees)', April 1888;
Ramparts of Paris', summer 1887; 'Olive Trees with Yellow Sky and Sun',
November 1889; 'Landscape with the Chateau of Auvers at Sunset', 1890;
'Cottages and Cypresses Reminisence of the North', March–April 1890.

Looking closely at many of Van Gogh's paintings, there are some wonderful combinations of subtle colours in contrast to the brighter, more vivid pictures. Here I have recorded some of these soft nuances of colour.

1 Straight lines of a variety of fabrics sewn close together: cotton, scrim, chiffon and polyester.

2 Short pieces of fabric laid down in a circular arrangement, moving to longer lengths and changing direction.

1 A variety of straight stitches.

2 A variety of straight stitches.

3 Cretan stitches with straight stitches in opposing directions.

4 Horizontal straight stitches.

5 Blocks of straight stitches.

6 Machine texture applied to a background with backstitch.

51

Textured Purse

I decided to use some of the textures explored to make some fabric for a small purse. I began by making a drawing of what I wanted the purse to look like. I then made a calico toile to test the pattern.

The purse is constructed from two circles, one set into the other. The top circle should be the correct size to fit a purchased metal purse frame, and the lower circle should have a semicircle cut out to fit the upper circle. To ensure that the outer seam would be neat and easy to sew to the reverse side, I backed the stitched pieces with a bright orange fabric to add a contrast lining to the inside of the purse. Both sides were made and completed before sewing together. The outside edge is decorated with a rat-tail cord and the holes around the purse frame are filled with small red beads. The stitching is done with a variety of cotton and silk threads in straight stitches and sorbello stitch.

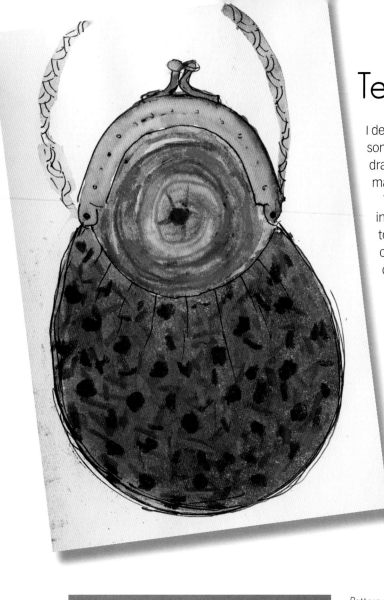

My initial drawing for the flat purse.

Pattern pieces form a calico toile to try out the design.

The finished project.

Further developments

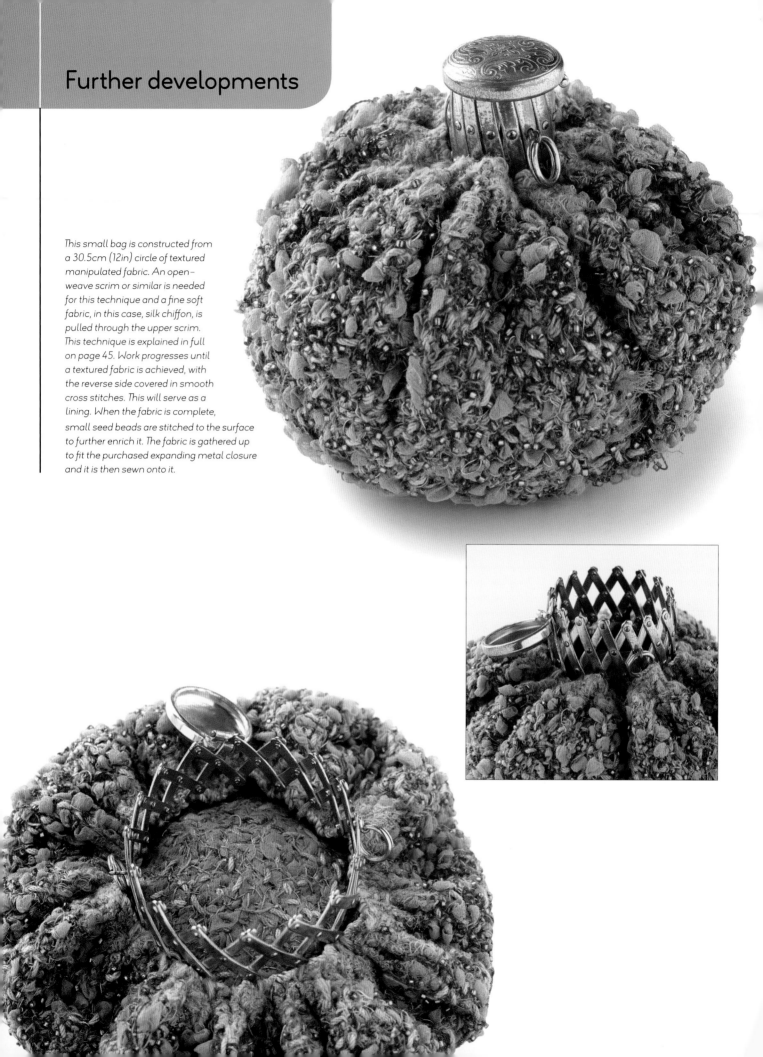

This small bag is constructed from a 30.5cm (12in) circle of textured manipulated fabric. An open-weave scrim or similar is needed for this technique and a fine soft fabric, in this case, silk chiffon, is pulled through the upper scrim. This technique is explained in full on page 45. Work progresses until a textured fabric is achieved, with the reverse side covered in smooth cross stitches. This will serve as a lining. When the fabric is complete, small seed beads are stitched to the surface to further enrich it. The fabric is gathered up to fit the purchased expanding metal closure and it is then sewn onto it.

Landscape With Tree

I was inspired by Van Gogh's landscapes and decided to create one of my own. I took photographs of the landscape around where I live and cut and pieced them together to create a design. The stitching was worked onto a dissolvable background and applied to a linen fabric after washing away the background. A further piece was constructed with fabric and stitching, again on a dissolvable background, and this was laid on top of the base stitching. The hedge on the skyline was made separately by machine and added with further stitching. The rough-textured foreground adds to the sense of distance and the tree brooch is attached to the panel to further enhance the image.

This brooch came from looking at the shape and form of the trees in Van Gogh's landscapes. The couched trunk and branches are stitched over a machined texture and I have added fringing.

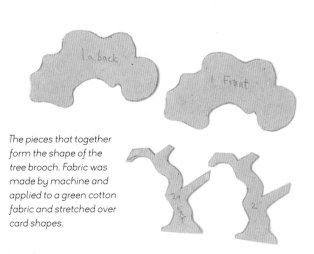

The pieces that together form the shape of the tree brooch. Fabric was made by machine and applied to a green cotton fabric and stretched over card shapes.

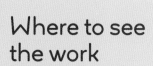

Kandinsky

Wassily Kandinsky was born in Moscow in 1866 and died in France in 1944. He was a European Russian, and was engaged in many aspects of art, although painting was his primary work. He initially qualified as a lawyer but gave this up to study art at the age of 30. He experimented with watercolour, gouache, tempera, woodcuts, drypoint, lithograph, murals, illustration, graphic design, typography, furniture, fashion, jewellery, porcelain, stage sets, creative writing, poetry and plays. Believing that art did not need to represent actual forms and objects, he defined a basic pictorial language of pure colours and forms and suggested what it could be made to communicate, and how this could be achieved. He believed that colours and forms could have an emotional impact on the viewer.

There was a constant duality in Kandinsky's art: it showed a romantic spirit and a love of humour on the one hand and a controlled, disciplined, meticulous manner on the other. He was isolated from his artistic contemporaries, and two aspects of his personality often clashed: his intuition and reason;

his spontaneous side and his need to be disciplined, calculated and precise. He was intensely emotional, but kept his feelings to himself. Kandinsky was influenced by the folklore of Old Russia, maintaining that it was the origin of his art, but he was also very European and settled in Paris, where he eventually became a French citizen.

He believed that all worthwhile art resulted from a compulsion that was irresistible, unconscious and therefore inaccessible to reason. 'Inner necessity' was what made him want to paint. He thought that painting should 'constantly aspire to the condition of music', as music, in his view, affects the senses more powerfully than any other art form.

Kandinsky was the first twentieth-century artist to create abstract art. His pictures contained shapes and colours, lines and geometric compositions influenced by the Bauhaus. His colours were bright and saturated and his art expressed the conflict between reason and 'inner necessity'.

'Colour is the keyboard. The eye is the hammer. The soul is the piano with its many strings.'

Wassily Kandinsky

Where to see the work

You can see Kandinsky's work in many locations, but larger collections are in the Stadtische Galerie in Lenbach, Munich; the Centre Georges Pompidou, Paris; the Guggenheim Museum and the Museum of Modern Art, New York; the Art Institute of Chicago; the State Tretyakov Gallery, Moscow and the Tate Modern, London.

56

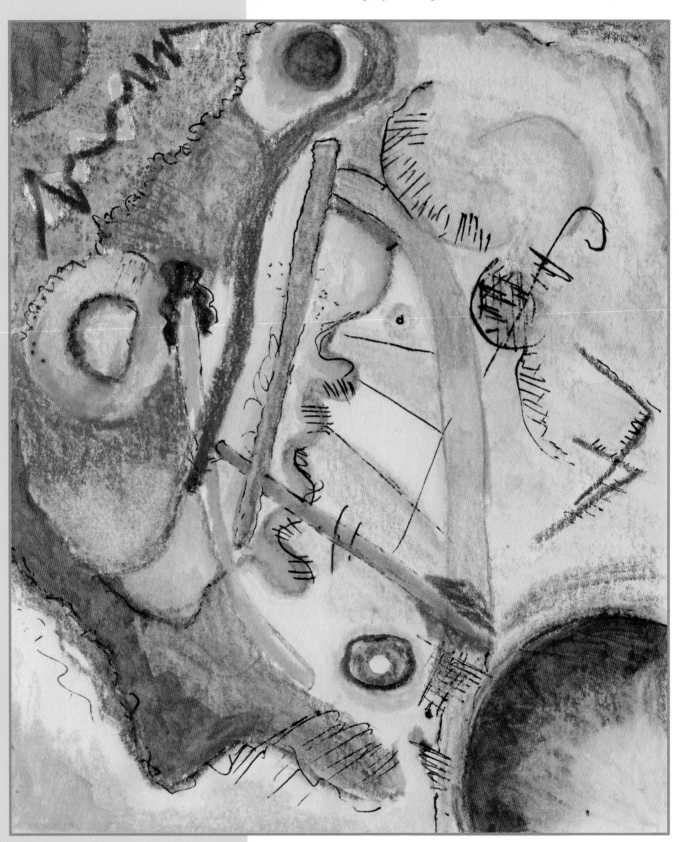

Reasons for choosing Kandinsky

I am drawn to Kandinsky's bright primary colours and use of line. I also like the rather quirky characters and the use of geometric shapes to make abstract compositions not based on reality.

I have concentrated on these elements and combined shape with line to create small structures and compositions. The individual components are joined together in various ways, making it unnecessary for them to be attached to a background; they can be free standing. The colours are strong and vibrant, often primary, and I saw this as an opportunity to make lots of small decorative items composed of all those bits and pieces that we textile artists collect in the hope that they will be useful one day.

The linear elements can be made from wires of various kinds, heavy string or thick threads for wavy lines and sticks or straws for straight and rigid lines.

The geometric shapes may be made from card covered with fabric, craft-weight interfacing or several layers of fabric bonded together until they become firm. I have subverted some electronic parts to be painted or decorated and become components within a composition, and tried to be playful in the shapes I have made in response to the musical aspects of Kandinsky's work. These shapes could be made into mobiles so that they hang in space and move as the air moves around them.

On this page are some lines and shapes I have recorded from Kandinsky's paintings. They have a spontaneity to them that I hope to capture in my own work.

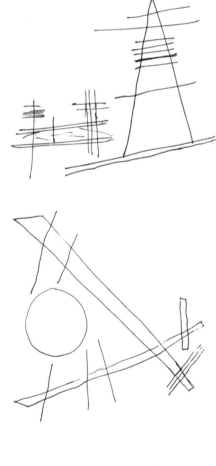

A collection of little structures randomly chosen from various Kandinsky paintings and reproduced in my sketchbook.

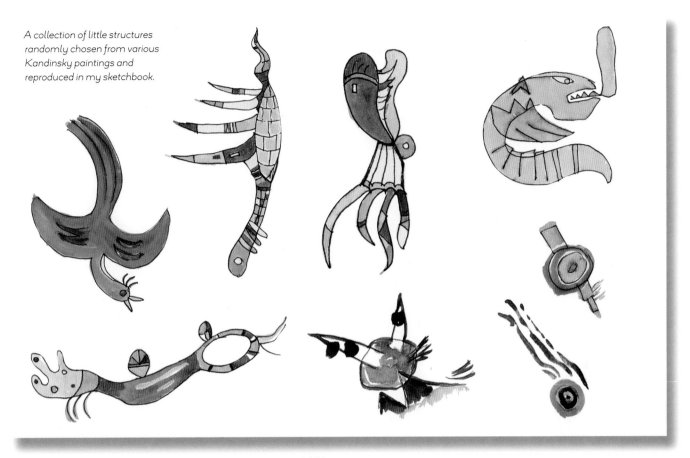

Below are some of my own line drawings. I was trying to tap into a childlike state to create some whimsical characters in the style of Kandinsky.

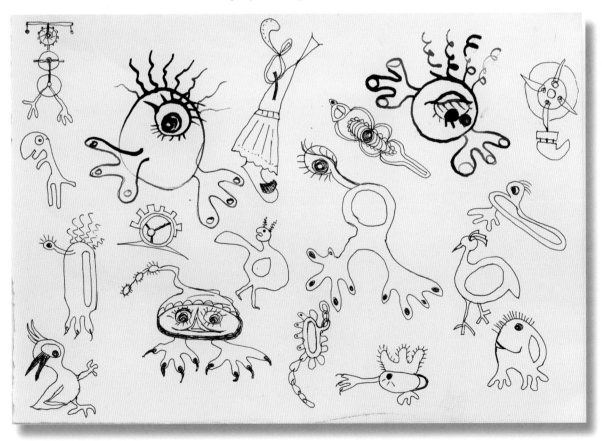

Design development

I began by making some drawings directly from Kandinsky's paintings. This enabled me to become acquainted with his work in more detail and to start to figure out some ideas of my own. It is all too easy just to copy the content of an artist's work and not to make your own response to it. Kandinsky's images of quirky little creatures appealed to me and I have attempted to draw my own imaginary birds and beasts. You need a child's eye view to achieve this, and to be abandoned in the way you develop shapes that are suggestive of animals or birds but are not lifelike.

Exercise

Try this: Take a circle and add a shape to it. Make a line run through it, meandering as it goes. Add an eye and some lashes or some feet with huge toes. The poem from Lewis Carroll's *Through the Looking-Glass* comes to mind with it's Jabberwock and slithy toves. What do they look like?
It takes some practice, but eventually ideas begin to form and these should be recorded with diagrams or thumbnail sketches.

To illustrate the exercise, I constructed a collage as a stepping-stone stage to making a three-dimensional character.

Exercise

This exercise exploits the use of vertical and horizontal space. It involves cutting shapes from the edge of a piece of paper or card and folding them back to the outside. If the paper is a different colour on the reverse side, it adds contrast. The exercise can be done by drawing very accurate geometrical shapes such as circles, squares or oblongs, or by cutting randomly into the paper, which gives a more dynamic and spontaneous quality to the cut shapes.

The exercise can be further developed by starting with an irregular shape and altering or reshaping the foldouts.

These ideas could serve as backgrounds to a series of geometric shapes laid on top, with or without space in between.

Further processes

It is worth taking time to consider the nature of shapes and to explore the extent of their diversity. Shapes may be geometric or amorphic. Geometric, rectilinear shapes are composed of mainly straight lines, as in squares and triangles, with a continuous line describing the extent of the shape. Circles and ovals are geometric shapes too with the same continuous line around them. They may be symmetrical or asymmetrical.

Amorphic shapes are irregular and abstract, and are also described by a continuous line. The outside edge of any shape, whether geometric or amorphic, need not be a solid line, but can be dotted, dashed or otherwise drawn with marks just close enough for the eye to register the shape. This type of line features in many of Kandinsky's paintings.

Designs of the 1950s featured shapes like these in furniture and fabrics. Boomerang shapes appeared across the decorative arts at this time.

Shapes may be shown as solid colour or simply an outline, and may be recognisable as familiar objects or purely abstract, with no discernable identity.

Within art, shapes may be used as a code to suggest meaning, without being too literal. They can also be simplified, as in the symbols used for road signs or musical notation.

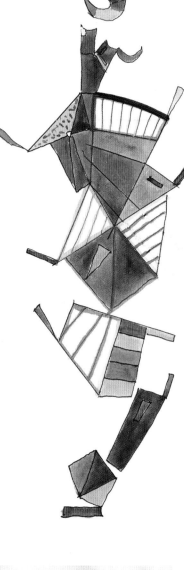

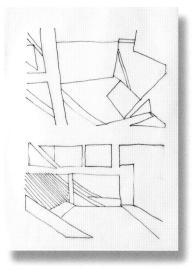

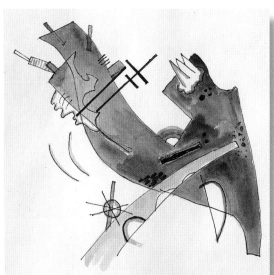

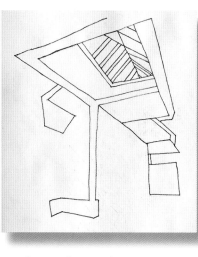

I have been inspired by Kandinsky's use of geometric and amorphic shape and have explored methods of using and combining these. I made some collages from a drawing and then took a section from these to develop further. Shapes can be combined to make new ones, or enlarged and joined with others of a different scale.

I used painted paper and cut out shapes with a scalpel. I filled these spaces with a contrasting coloured paper, stuck from behind. A stitched version of this can be seen on page 66.

A drawing made from Kandinsky's work, 'With the Arrow', 1943.

Using found objects

I have worked with all manner of found objects in my response to Kandinsky's work. I show some of them here, as they are not listed in the materials chapter.

Card covered with fabric forms the basis of many of the items that I have explored. The type of card will depend on how large the shape is. The larger the shape, the stronger the card should be but this of course makes it more difficult to cut, so it is advisable to keep angles and curves as simple as possible. I use offcuts of mountboard or medium-weight grey board in this instance. If you are covering a small shape, card that is easy to cut with scissors should be adequate. It is also reasonable in this case to use craft-weight interfacing as an alternative. I have a drawer full of cardboard that I have kept for recycling so that I always have a variety of types to choose from when I am exploring ideas.

Wire of all types and thicknesses is great for binding, threading and joining. I use paper-covered wire, floristry wires, cake decorating wire and copper and jewellery wire.

Washers come in metal, plastic, rubber and sometimes fabric. They can be wrapped or bound with thread. I have also covered the larger, flatter ones with fabric. They can be threaded, put one on top of another or small ones inside large ones, depending on the requirements of your design.

Electronic parts can be used to decorate or add details. These items come in many forms, some with small pieces of coloured plastic attached, others with small holes that are useful for threading.

I have discovered shrink rubber tubing, normally used to enclose wires, and have used it to trap thread and bits of fabric within it. Fill the tube with thread by passing it through in a needle. When you have enough thread in the tube, heat it with a craft heat gun, making sure that you hold the tube with tweezers to keep fingers out of harm's way. After only a few seconds, you can see the rubber shrink, tightening around the thread within the tube. The tubing is available in a variety of sizes and colours, although I have only used black.

A polystyrene oval shape is covered with fabric and sits on a base constructed from fabric-covered card and a tea-light container, also covered with fabric. Electronic wires decorate the head.

A polystyrene ball is painted with acrylic paint and covered with buttonhole rings made on a couronne stick. Wire wrapped with black thread is twisted and holds a small polystyrene ball decorated with an eyelash and eyeball. A strip of metal subverted from electronics is threaded with a cord and has added tufts of thread throughout its length. The structure sits on a foot made from card covered with fine black leather with a suggestion of toes added with tiny buttonhole rings.

In addition, a leather needle is useful as it will go through tougher fabrics more easily than an ordinary one because of its triangular cross section. This means that it has three cutting edges, so it glides through the fabric. Strong waxed linen or cotton thread is good for securing sections or parts of construction together. This is available from bookbinding suppliers.

A couronne stick is used for making buttonhole rings. This is a wooden stick with notches at intervals for making rings of different sizes. Thread is wound around the stick several times and then covered with buttonhole stitch. Couronne sticks are available in several sizes from specialist haberdashery suppliers.

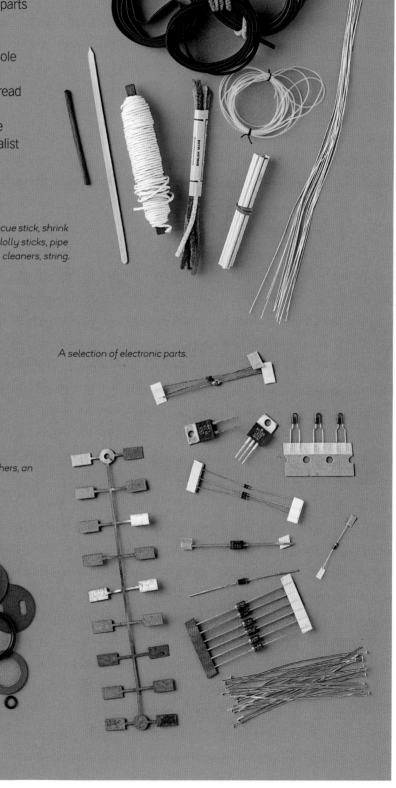

Clockwise from left: matchstick, barbecue stick, shrink tubing, plastic wire, cake icing wires, lolly sticks, pipe cleaners, string.

A selection of electronic parts.

Clockwise from top: a collection of plastic and metal washers, an adapter, polystyrene oval and false eyelashes.

Stitched pieces

Working from the design on page 62, I have made a stitched version of this using balsa wood. This is very easy to cut with a craft knife or scalpel and allows a needle to pass through it for stitching. The structure is on several levels with stitching added onto the surface of the wood. I have used a needlelace stitch to fill the spaces and some lines of buttonholed thread. Although this structure is free-standing, it could easily be stitched to a background fabric.

Three small structures developed from shapes seen in Kandinsky's paintings. I have used fabric-covered card, painted balsa wood, painted interfacing, buttonhole rings and buttonhole stitch to create them.

Inspired by the drawing on page 58, I have stitched this abstract design, using straight stitches to colour in the shapes. The circle is a wrapped curtain ring applied to the background, which is randomly marked with fabric paint. A painted cocktail stick is couched down next to the black chequered pattern.

These two brooches are stitched with lines and shapes inspired by the abstractions seen in Kandinsky's work.

Making structures

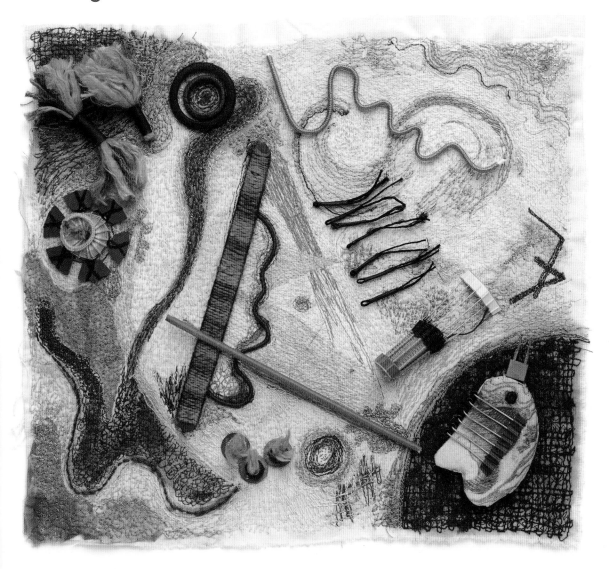

Here I have explored making small structures and stitching onto electronic parts. Some are shapes with added details using covered washers, painted sticks and wires wrapped with thread, small-scale buttonhole stitch and plumes of fluffy thread. Some are secured with heat-shrink tubing and others stuck into the centres of tea-light candles. These are shown on a machine stitched background and could become part of a panel or picture.

Covering card with fabric

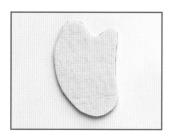

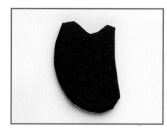

1 Add a layer of fine felt or interfacing to the card shape.

2 Stretch fabric over the top and secure with glue.

3 Cover a piece of interfacing with fabric to back the first shape and join both pieces together with oversewing.

Abstract Construction with Line and Shape

The finished piece. Working with circles, squares, triangles and lines, I decided to separate the background from these shapes and to introduce some dimension. The component parts are joined to each other and the structure is fixed into a frame to float against a plain white background.

68

Detail of the finished piece. A large plastic washer is covered with black cotton fabric, with a smaller stitched one in the centre. A set of false eyelashes is fixed to the edge, and there are wrapped sticks and wires and painted, stitched interfacing.

Detail showing painted barbecue sticks, wrapped lolly sticks, wound wire beads and wrapped wire.

Austrian artist, Friedrensreich Hundertwasser (1928–2000) was born in Vienna. He developed his artistic skills early in life and had a strong individual style. He was educated at a Montessori school where his self-directed learning was inspired by the colour and organic shapes in nature. He was fascinated by spirals and had a dislike of straight lines, which he described as 'the devil's tools' and 'godless and immoral'. He felt that we had lost our connection with nature by forcing ourselves to live in square boxes and he hated the grid system of conventional architecture and the mechanical output of industrial production. This conviction of his demanded a life in accordance with the laws of nature and led to his campaigns for the right to create individual structures for the preservation of the natural habitat. His preference was for organic imagery with fluidity of line and shape. This is seen in his ideas for architecture where he developed new shapes: a spiral house, eye-slit house and high-rise meadow house. These buildings were conceived with environmental issues central to their design. He viewed windows as eyes and as the bridge between inside and outside.

His work has been described as Transautomatism, a kind of Surrealism, focusing on fantasy. His work was not limited to architecture: he also made graphic work, lithographs, silk screen printing, etching and woodcuts. His tapestries were made freehand without templates, as he wanted to breathe life into them rather than producing a soulless copy of a design. Hundertwasser's temperament meant that he did not want to be constrained by any framework, so that he could further his aim to restore beauty and romanticism to everyday life.

Much of Hundertwasser's work is based on architecture and dominated by linear structures, with bright, intense colour, often using complementary colours with the addition of gold and silver, pasted on in a thin foil. The work has simple organic form, with the same kinds of shape repeated again and again. Lines meander around shape, eyes loom out of landscapes and trees adorn rooftops.

Opposite

This drawing of mine was inspired by a section of a mixed media painting by Hundertwasser, 'The End of Greece', 1964. '

'the devil's tools'

'Godless and immoral'

'the rotten foundation of our doomed civilization'

Hundertwasser's view of straight lines

Where to see the work

A large collection of work may be seen at the Museum Hundertwasser in Vienna, designed by the artist, Kunst Haus Wien. Buildings designed or altered by Hundertwasser include the Rosenthal Factory, Selb, Germany; the Mierke Grain Silo, Krems, Austria; the Rupertinum Museum of Modern Art, Saltzburg, Austria; and Hundertwasser's House in Vienna, Austria.

Reasons for choosing Hundertwasser

I am inspired by Hundertwasser's linear style. I like the sinuous contour lines that wrap around simple shapes and the way that they expand and shrink in width as they meander across the picture. I also rather agree with him about straight lines being unimaginative and dull. A line with a degree of wobble seems to have more character and expression.

The colour is uplifting, often bold and primary, with strong contrasts and outlines.

'I love the rather mysterious, eccentric imagery, with eyes and faces that loom up out of landscapes.'

This drawing of mine was inspired by a section of a mixed-media painting by Hundertwasser, 'Zwolle, Zwolle,' 1964.

Working from the inspiration

I made some drawings directly from various paintings chosen, because they suggested ideas either for stitching or for colour combinations. There was always the potential for them to develop into ideas for finished pieces. This was also a way of acquainting myself with the artist's work, and became a study of shape, colour and pattern. While I did this, I was considering how I might use this inspiration. These small drawings suggested building up the surface or cutting back.

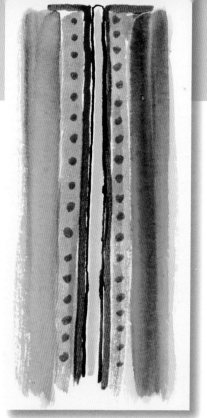

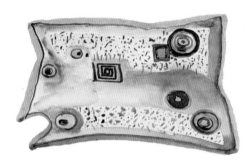

'These drawings reminded me of maps, with their contours and blocks created by buildings, trees and fences dividing the spaces.'

A sketchbook page of small drawings taken from a variety of Hundertwasser's paintings.

First development process

It is a good idea to make some drawings using inspiration from the artist's work, as shown on the previous page. That way it is possible to understand more about the subject matter, colour palette and composition.

With this information in mind, try the following exercise for making a painting from memory about a place or journey that is familiar to you. It could be a map of your town or village, or the journey to work. To begin, tape a medium-sized brush to the end of a garden cane, and take a large piece of cartridge paper; about A3 size. Put the paper on the floor and work with acrylic paints. Hold the cane at the end rather than lower down as you would if you were working on a normal surface with your usual brush. Choose a palette of bright colours; not necessarily realistic. For example, buildings may be pink or yellow and roads may be red or purple. Be careful not to stir up your colours, thus creating muddy colours, and do not thin your paint too much; keep it thick.

Paint imaginary lines and shapes to suggest architecture. It will be difficult to be very detailed, because the long-handled brush will force you to simplify. When you are satisfied with your picture, leave it to dry. When it is ready, you can add detail or refine areas with either water-soluble crayons or oil crayons, working on a normal table surface. You should end up with a large painting depicting an imaginary place or journey.

When the painting is dry, turn the paper over and walk away from it for a while. When you return to it, cut it up randomly into about six uneven sections, without looking at the picture. It is a good idea to make the sections either square or oblong, though the sides may slope a little. Avoid creating sharp, obtuse angles to the pieces. Cutting up your picture will give you a selection of small compositions that have been randomly created, thus avoiding those difficult decisions about where to place colour and shape.

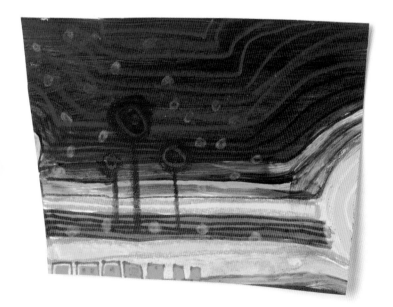

Turn the pieces over and examine what you have made. These mini compositions can be used as they are for stitching or for further development, and most should be workable. If you get a couple that don't work or that you don't like, use them as design paper for cutting up and applying to the other designs or to new ones. If you want to preserve your picture before cutting, you could either photocopy or photograph it.

Choose one piece that you like for stitching, and put it aside. The remaining compositions will be used to create designs with raised areas or could be developed into boxes or other items.

'Try to be adventurous with your colours and avoid playing safe.'

These small compositions and the ones opposite are the result of the exercise outlined on page 74.

Further processes

Collage

Collage is a method of piecing and patching and adding different layers to a design. The layers may be added on or taken away, leaving holes or spaces. I have cut up some of my drawings and mounted parts of them onto different thicknesses of card. Here are some ideas:

- You could cut a particular section out, mount it onto foam board to give depth and then place it back in your composition.
- You could create depth by cutting out a shape, making a box around it and then replacing it so that you look into it.
- You could create some finer details by adding raised lines with string or rolled paper beads with small shapes stuck on top.
- Wires could be added with shapes at the end.
- Spaces could be created by cutting a drawing apart and rejoining it using strips of paper, small sticks or shaped card.

I collaged onto these drawings by cutting them apart and mounting the cut pieces onto foam card, then re-piecing.

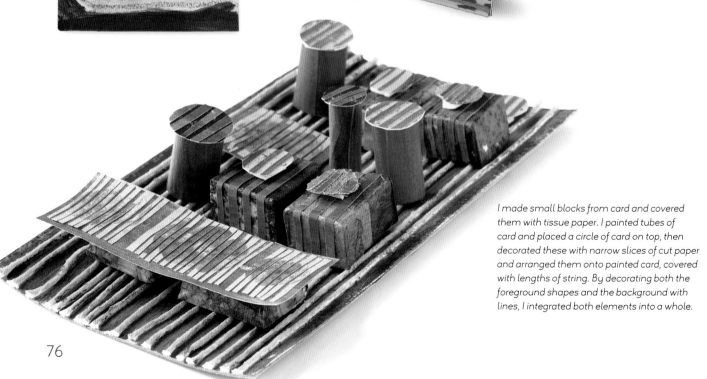

I made small blocks from card and covered them with tissue paper. I painted tubes of card and placed a circle of card on top, then decorated these with narrow slices of cut paper and arranged them onto painted card, covered with lengths of string. By decorating both the foreground shapes and the background with lines, I integrated both elements into a whole.

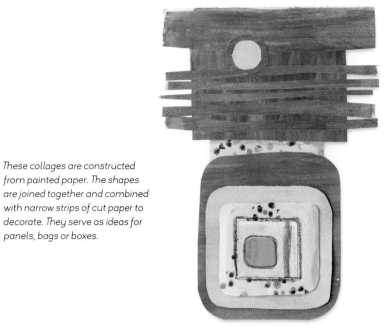

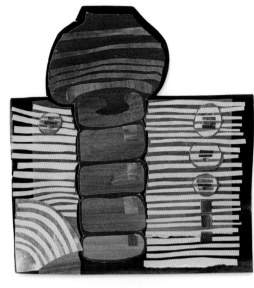

These collages are constructed from painted paper. The shapes are joined together and combined with narrow strips of cut paper to decorate. They serve as ideas for panels, bags or boxes.

A series of small blocks are combined together and placed at different heights. Some are raised onto foam card and some flat.

thods of raising the surface. A rectangular
rm is made from folded card. A triangle
e same way is placed above it. Narrow
d are arranged across the open box to
he painted stripes on the background.
ard cut into a spiral is placed into the
e house shape in the centre is made in the
A rectangular box made from folded card
oside down to create a platform. Further
ld be added to this. On the right, a narrow
card is folded to create a rectangular
e like a maze and fixed to the background.

Raised areas

Using patterns from Hundertwasser's paintings,
I developed some raised areas.
a) I made small dots by setting coloured circles
of paper on top of a small piece of foam board.
b) I used the same idea with dots here but
raised them higher by setting the dots onto a
piece of rolled paper.
c) I raised the purple zigzag line onto a
piece of string to lift it above the lines of the
background.
d) Three small arched shapes are set back
from the drawing so that you look into the
spaces. To do this, I cut out the shapes and
made a narrow strip of thin card to fit around
the edge of the shape. I fixed this in place
temporarily with masking tape. I made a more
permanent join by using thin paper over the
shape, spreading onto the background.

a b c d

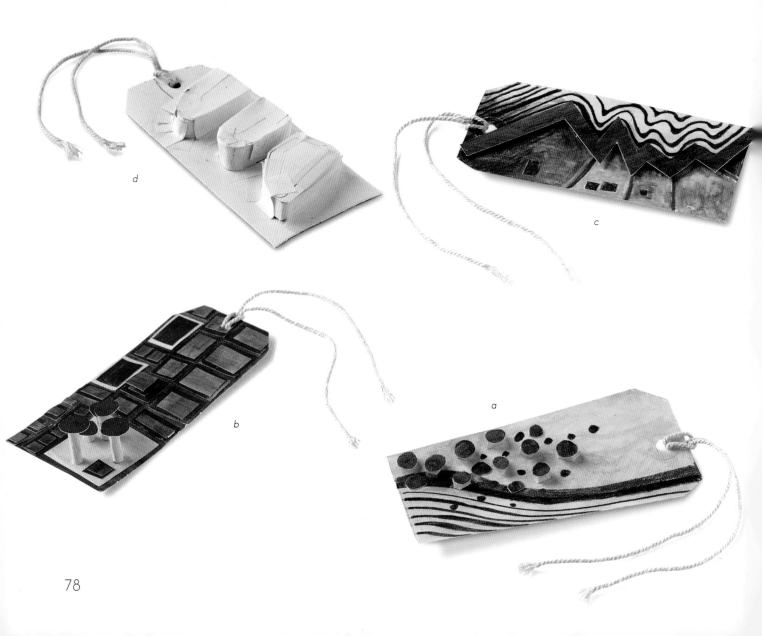

d

c

b

a

Torn paper drawing

I use this method to turn a flat, lifeless drawing into something more painterly. Working from an image that I have drawn, I recreate it using tiny pieces of torn coloured paper. Depending on which direction you tear the paper, you will get some pieces that have a white line on the edge. These can really add an extra ingredient to your design. If you don't want all the white edges showing, you can re-colour them with crayons or paint.

I roughly mark the basic shapes of the design and then fill them with the torn paper. If I have coloured the paper myself, I will get all the little irregular marks that appear on the painted paper. I usually make sure that I have not painted the paper smoothly so that there are many small irregularities of colour and texture on the surface. In this way, when I come to use it for this technique, I get a random spread of surface variation.

The tiny pieces of torn paper are glued to the paper background. To do this, I put the glue onto the background, drop the torn paper on top and smooth it down. If the background paper is a suitable colour, you will not need to cover the whole surface – you can allow gaps of background paper to show through. This may be a blending colour or a complete contrast; darker, lighter or a different colour altogether.

When it comes to transferring this into stitching, each small piece of paper equates to a small block of stitches or tiny fragment of fabric. This is ideal for backgrounds.

Further developments

Ideas for boxes

Hundertwasser's work inspires dimensional developments. His quirky shapes in odd settings suggest box shapes and I have been inspired to explore his work using dimension as the primary outcome. I have looked for unusual shapes and tried to imagine them as dimensional objects with unconventional surfaces and appendages. Profiles are not symmetrical and they may be raised up on stilts or platforms. Unlikely sections may have openings and windows may become eyes. Gather all your ideas together on a page in your sketchbook and record them without judgement. At first some ideas may seem ridiculous but often what might have been rejected on these grounds, may take on a new guise when seen among other suggestions. Allow your subconscious mind to work on them for a while and then when you see them with fresh eyes, you may find that you can develop them into something workable.

When I start planning a new piece of work, I like to have time to play with ideas first without letting practicalities take over. When I get a design that I like, I will decide at that point how best to make it.

These paper collages are ideas for boxes. My next stage will be to make a mock-up in card so that I can work out what the problems will be and then find a solution.

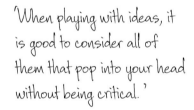

'When playing with ideas, it is good to consider all of them that pop into your head without being critical.'

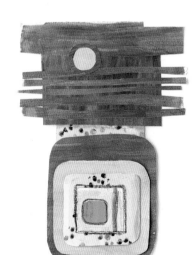

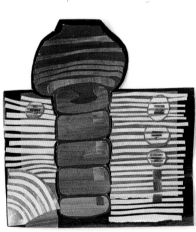

These six drawings were made from a random selection of circular motifs seen in a variety of Hundertwasser's paintings. I am drawn to circles, and there are plenty to choose from when exploring the work of this imaginative artist. Some are faces that loom out of buildings, and others are found among the rich patterning of his imagery. Windows and trees are attached to the linear landscape with small details that seem to fix these shapes into the composition.

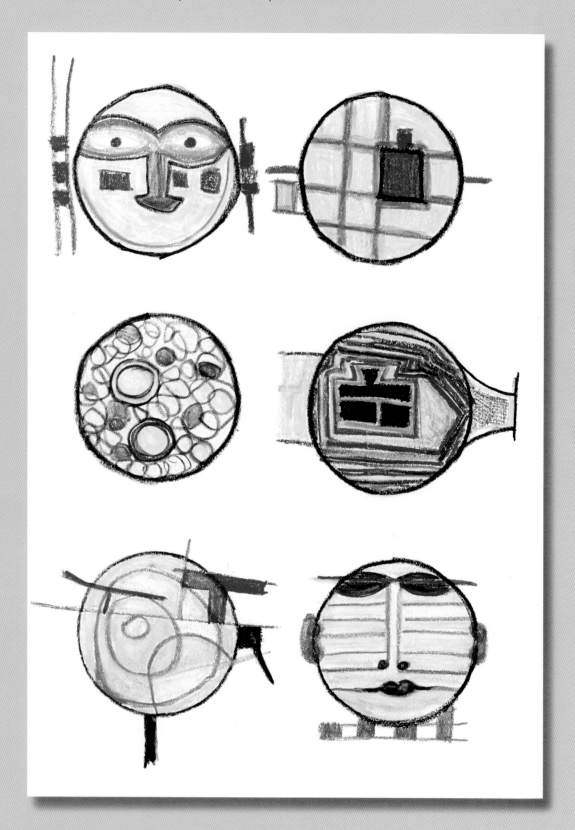

Stitching

The rich and varied surface of Hundertwasser's work just cries out to be stitched. Since there are so many lines and outlines, couching is an obvious choice, as it is a linear technique but has several variations to add interest. Just using the vibrant colours seen in Hundertwasser's paintings gives exciting possibilities for combinations.

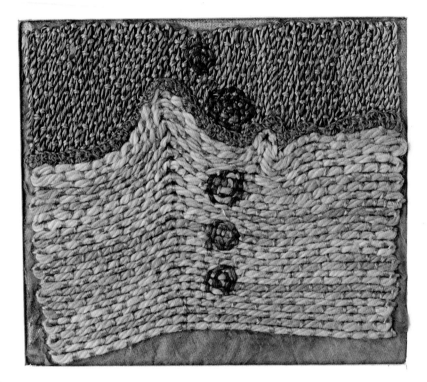

Couching

Cotton thread is contrasted with a variegated rayon, and they are set at right angles to each other. Simple couching is used with one line of buttonhole stitch to separate them. Backstitch circles have been worked on top.

Darning

I have used the torn paper drawing (page 79) as a basis for darning (right), a stitching technique that lends itself to painterly interpretation. It takes a while to blend areas together in this way, but the resulting effect is worthwhile.

Darning is best done on an openweave fabric, as this enables thick or uneven threads, or even torn fabric strips, to be sewn through it. I used fabric paint to mark out the main areas of the design so that it would not matter if some background fabric was seen, as it would blend with the thread colour. I applied some of the coloured shapes with fine fabrics and then worked the darning on top. I worked vertically and horizontally with running stitch, taking the needle under and over lines of stitching, weaving the threads through each other to create a surface. The dark lines outlining shapes followed the direction of the shape.

Dimensional samples

You can create a dimensional surface using a number of different techniques. Here are some ideas.

- Foam board wrapped with fabric can be applied to a background. The fabric may be stitched first, or after it is in place.

- A narrow piece of card covered with fabric or stitching can be set on its edge, making a raised line. Fine metal mesh may be used for this too and can take a machine stitch. Slip stitch this to the background. The wider it is, the more support it will need so that it remains firmly upright.

- Other types of padding can be used either to raise up stitching or to make a fabric shape. Use felt in layers according to the height that is required, or lay a foundation of stitching to pad further stitching on top.

- String in various thicknesses can be couched down and more stitching worked on top.

- Found objects could be painted or have stitching added, for example, rubber, metal or plastic washers, small pieces of wood or dowel can be incorporated into the work.

- Taking away is perhaps more of a challenge. Layers may be built up by cutting back through a pile of several fabrics layered together. Edges may be turned in to neaten or left raw for a softer effect. If more dimension is required, a backing in the form of craft-weight interfacing or card may be covered with fabric and layered shape upon shape.

- To neaten a hole or space, first tack around the space. Cut away the centre fabric, leaving enough to turn under the edges. Snip into any corners or curves to enable the fabric to lie tightly against the edge. It is worth remembering that if the fabric is on the bias, it will have more stretch. Fix by stitching if using interfacing, or use a fabric glue stick for card.

- Remember that linings for boxes or other open shapes need to be fractionally smaller than the outside measurements and ideally the fabric should be cut on the bias.

When making complex dimensional objects, time should be taken to work out an order of work. Some stages need to be completed before others can be done. Working from the inside to outside can work sometimes but not always, and careful measurement is often needed for an accurate finish.

Flat brooch

This brooch was worked by machine. The stitching was made to fit the shape exactly. I covered a backing of card with yellow fabric and sewed the machined fabric to this. The machined fabric was neatened with the addition of a fine cord around the edge.

Dimensional brooch

Straight stitch and chain stitch worked onto yellow silk forms the centre of this brooch. A buttonhole ring is applied in the centre of the triangle. The edging is constructed from fine metal mesh folded in half to make a firm lip around the shape. It is first machined together and then wrapped with a pink silk thread. The backing is foam board covered with yellow silk fabric with a brooch clip attached before construction. The rim is firmly sewn to the backing with a strong thread and finished with machine- and hand-wrapped wire over the top.

Sample book

Stitch samples

Samples of stitches that I have used for the work in this chapter are presented in a folder format with pockets for the individual samples, which are mounted on card. Each one is worked with a small section of design so that you can see what the stitches look like in practice. This also gives them coherence as a set.

a

b

c

d

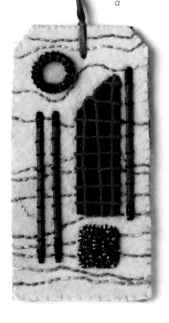

a) Padding *I used padding with felt, a rubber washer and a piece of balsa wood painted black, with wrapped stitches. Stitches are worked over the top of the padding material. Thick string and card could also be used together with any found object if it gives the shape and height needed.*

b) Filling stitches by machine *Free running, side to side zigzag, and couching stitces were used.*

c) Cords *A variety of cords are laid onto a design. They include machined cord, ribbon and knitting tape threaded through with wire. This is a bit tricky to do but it enables you to create a shape and couch it to the background fabric.*

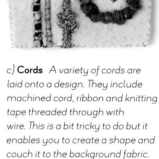

d) Minced fabric *This is a method of creating texture and has a painterly effect. Tiny fragments of varied fabrics are laid onto a background, which is painted or dyed with a suitable colour and tone to blend with them. I usually make this by machine, gradually adding small pieces of fabric and sewing them down using free running stitch and a blending coloured thread. In this sample I have sewn the pieces by hand, securing them with a seeding stitch and changing the colour throughout as appropriate. Some of the stitches are whipped. This is done with a thicker thread that is threaded around the straight stitch over and over again until the length of the stitch is covered. I have used very thick thread but also some finer ones to give contrast. I have also included French knots for further texture. Minced fabric is a good method for backgrounds and decorative stitching can be worked on top, provided that the working thread is not too thick.*

e   f   g   h

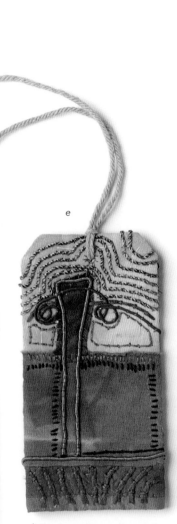

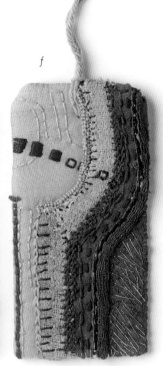

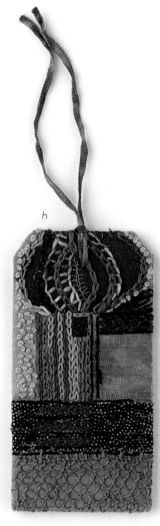

e) **Couching** This can be used to fill shapes or to outline them and the technique is an obvious choice for work inspired by Hundertwasser as so much of his work includes lines. They appear as texture when laid close together and as they meander around shapes, they vary in width, narrowing and expanding along their length. A variety of threads are couched onto a background of coloured shapes. Cotton, rayon and gimp are sewn down with finer threads. The holding stitches are small and are placed about 3mm (1/8in) apart. The spacing may vary depending on what type of thread is being couched. For example, rayon is a slippery thread and can lift and slide if the holding stitches are not close together enough, but cotton or linen threads will lie against their background more easily. Contrast is achieved by varying the type of thread and the spacing of stitches.

f) **Hand stitches** For this sample I have worked raised stem, raised chain, satin stitch, buttonhole, chain, threaded running and cross hatching with a fine thread.

g) **Darning** A painterly effect can be achieved using this technique. I have worked it here in a loose and random manner. Threads in a variety of colours have been darned into a loosely woven background fabric and blended together. Not all the stitches are sewn through the fabric. Some are threaded through worked stitches and sit on the surface of the fabric. The length of stitch also varies. In addition, I have placed small pieces of fabric onto the background prior to stitching. These are placed where the shapes in the design are small and fiddly and the running stitches are darned across them, blending them into the texture. There is also a couched line where the design requires a definite line that would be difficult to work as a darned line.

h) **Filling stitches by hand** Here I have used buttonhole, chain and French knots.

Book and pockets

I made a book to hold the stitch sample cards. Three pieces of 3mm (¹⁄₈in) grey board were cut to size to make the cover; two for the front and back and one narrow piece for the spine. I covered the side that was to be the outside with thin felt to cushion it. The cover textile was made using appliquéd shapes based on my drawings, stitched mainly by machine with hand stitch over the top. I couched cords and added running stitch and straight stitches to finish. When placing the boards on the decorative textile, I left a space between the pieces so that the book would close properly.

The inside of the cover is a polyester fabric backed with a medium-weight interfacing. The pockets are printed cotton. I applied these to the lining together with the decorative top edges before I joined the lining to the cover. This was slip stitched in place by hand. A machine cord wraps around the book to hold it closed.

The outside of the sample book, flattened out.

The sample book shown closed with its decorative cord.

The sample book shown open with the stitch sample cards in their pockets.

Square Box

For this box, I wanted to use circles based on the drawings on page 81 (see right) and as a circle fits into a square well, this made a simple design plan. The detail is in the surface patterning. The box is bright and vibrant, following in Hundertwasser's colour palette with a primary red felt lining contrasting with the yellow outside. It is made with a mixture of machine- and hand-stitched techniques.

I first made the circles using foam board as a base to cover with fabric. I made the sides and base from plywood, with the corners lined with black felt. The panels for the sides have a yellow on yellow free-machined texture with a different circular design sewn onto each side. I added couching to anchor the design to its surround. I used archival glue to paste the side panels to the wooden structure.

The lid has a rising lining so that it fits flush with the sides of the box. The top is decorated with a padded raised centre surrounded with machine texture made separately on a dissolvable background. Pieces of the same machine texture are arranged over the top to add further dimension.

The base is made of MDF and the feet are wooden cupboard knobs screwed to the base and painted black.

Each side of the box has a different design in the centre.

The box without its lid, showing the red felt lining.

Lid detail.

88

The finished square box.

Box on Stilts

The sides of this box are made from one length of fabric, so that only one seam is necessary. I added the lining first when the fabric was still flat.

Using archival glue, I stuck card pieces to a length of interfacing with a small space between each one so that the piece could fold into the box shape. This gives a bit of padding to the inside under the lining. The lining was then stretched over the card and fixed top and bottom. I then sewed the seam to join the sides using a curved needle.

The outside decoration was then made in one piece. Red and yellow fabrics were pieced together for the background and the detail was added to this by hand and machine stitch. It was fitted around the box when complete. Additional decoration was then added. I sewed on fabric-covered interfacing and painted sticks to make the stilts. These stand proud of the base, and I wrapped the ends with black fabric and secured them with stitching. The lid is soft so that it takes on the shape of the top of the box. The base is made separately, covered with machine-textured fabric and hand-stitched on using a curved needle.

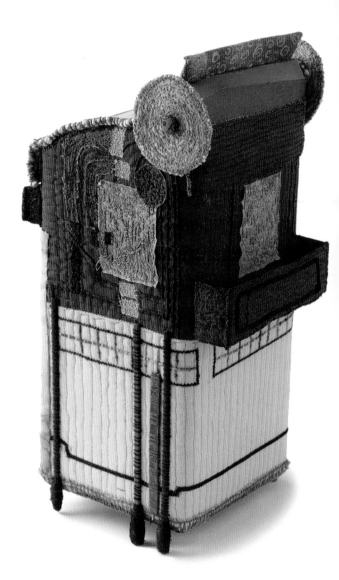

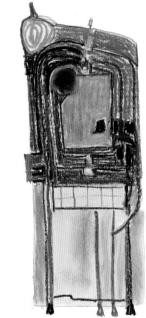

Various faces of the Box on Stilts and the drawing that inspired it.

Morandi

The work of Italian artist Giorgio Morandi (1890–1964) depicts the simple beauty of light on forms with subtle colouration and deft brush work, capturing the essence of simple objects and familiar landscapes.

Morandi was born in 1890 in Bologna, Italy, where he spent his entire life, with the exception of one trip to Switzerland in 1956. He was influenced by Classical Italian painting but also had a life-long interest in the work of French artist, Paul Cézanne. Morandi's work is considered to belong to the modern art genre of reduction and abstraction. His themes were still life and landscape and his primary concern was to record what he was seeing. Being face to face with his subject was of utmost importance. Everything he painted was about the visual experience. He painted the view from his studio window and the same everyday objects such as bottles and tins, time and time again, with a rigour that characterised the precision of the man and his life. He captured the particular texture of Bologna, with delicate colours of old plaster and the skin of a mushroom.

Morandi used space, light, colour and form to transform what he saw into what he painted. He placed the objects in such a way as to suggest relationships between them and quiet conversations from shape to shape. Sometimes in the paintings they are so close together that they almost merge into one shape, with the background changing places with the object. He divided the background into thirds to create changing perceptions of space, form and surface.

Morandi's paintings are surprisingly small; when I saw some of them in an exhibition, they were an average of 30 x 40cm (11 x 15¾in) in size. I wanted my works inspired by Morandi to reflect this intimacy.

I have used the still life theme, one that I have touched on in my earlier work, and a neutral palette inspired by the subtlety of Morandi's colours. He used greys, some slightly yellow, some verging on lavender, others tinged with blue, pink or green; as well as backgrounds of mink or mushroom and objects depicted in whites, creams, browns and duck-egg blue. There is an absence of stark contrasts in his work; these are rather soft and gentle, with line and texture supporting form. The paint is thin, creating liquid washes which seem to add to the rather ethereal quality of the colour.

'His paintings have a stillness about them, a calmness that supports contemplation and suggests stability and presence.'

Where to see the work

Morandi did not travel much during his lifetime so the main place to see his work is the Museo Morandi in Bologna. Other museums and art galleries have a few of his works, including the Museum of Modern Art in New York, and in the UK the Sainsbury Centre of Visual Arts, Norwich; the University of East Anglia; Birmingham Museums Trust; Estorick Collection of Italian Art, London; Tate Gallery, London; and the National Gallery of Scotland.

My version of Morandi's 'Still Life, 1963'.

'His objects and landscapes exude a
mellow and intimate serenity.'

Inspiration and drawings

I chose some small objects – jugs and a vase such as Morandi painted – and began by drawing them in a variety of arrangements, using chalk pastels. Pastels have a soft, muted quality that I feel is right for this artist's work. It is possible to soften and blend colour by rubbing with the finger or a piece of soft paper. This helps to blur edges and lines and one colour can be worked into another to create the tertiary colours seen in Morandi's paintings. The drawing process allowed me to become familiar with the objects I had chosen so that I could recreate them and explore the shapes and surfaces using collage.

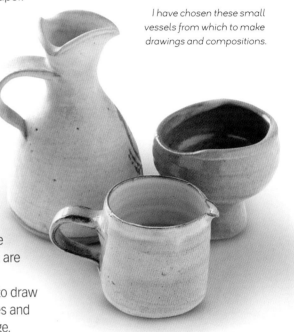

I have chosen these small vessels from which to make drawings and compositions.

Arrangements of the chosen objects can be altered and varied depending on how you want to present them. Morandi placed his vessels close together in tight groups, the same arrangement often appearing in more than one painting, but with subtle differences. He placed the objects on a flat surface indicated by a change in the colour of the background surface. A single line separates foreground from background. In some of the paintings, the objects seem to be perilously close to the edge of the table or shelf that they are sitting on. In others there appears to be much more depth, with the line indicating the edge of the surface that the objects are on skimming the tops of the bottle or jar.

It is worth taking the time to vary the placement of your objects and to draw them again and again in slightly different positions. Play with sight lines and edges and see what the effect is when you vary the depth of the image.

A page from my sketchbook showing the chosen vessels in different arrangements and drawn with a variety of media.

Inspired by Morandi

'There is no better way to understand an object than by spending time drawing it.'

I decided to try to capture the subtle quality of the form using techniques and fabric types for my drawings that would allow me to bring the shapes in and out of focus. I experimented with recording my objects by first pasting fine gauze and scrim on to cartridge paper, blending them together with gesso. I added a few bits of objects and then painted the image with watered-down ink. I tried to make the surface slightly raised and to keep edges soft and blurred, using quiet neutral colour.

Pastels are an ideal choice for delicate blends of colour. I like them in this context as they give a matt surface with soft edges to the shapes. You can rub the colour back with a soft cloth to lift the chalk off the surface but you will still need to treat it with a spray fixative

A drawing using wax and ink wash.

Images on uneven surfaces

Morandi's surfaces are very thinly painted, with the brush strokes very evident. I have tried to create this soft effect by creating backgrounds with scrim and muslin, someimes with added paper pulp to alter the surface and soften edges. I was looking for surfaces that would give some textural interest but would be delicate and soft-toned.

I wanted to achieve an uneven surface where the image comes and goes, and rubbing in paper pulp obscures some of the drawn lines or other detail. Gesso works in the same way. You can apply it before or after drawing or both. I use it to correct detail and positioning within a drawing, or to knock back colour or texture. It is useful for adding texture too if it is applied coarsely or with a palette knife.

Pots of gesso and paper pulp, a palette knift used for scraping on gesso and paper pulp, plastic cards for scraping and a print roller (brayer).

A drawing of the small vessels using gesso, scrim and acrylics.

A drawing using inks, paper and pulp, on cartridge paper covered with scrim.

Background samples

Fine, almost transparent fabrics can give soft effects when placed under or over stitching. I used these materials for the design development as well as for the stitch samples so that the two stages are very closely linked. These background samples show a variety of treatments using gesso, fine gauze, builder's scrim, paint and stitching.

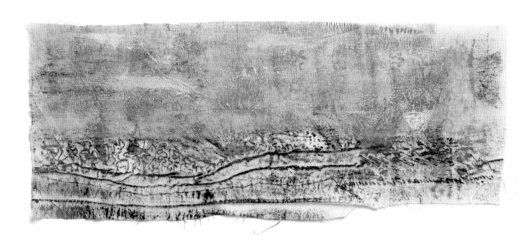

Washed calico, stitched first with seeding and long straight stitches. Printing ink in blue and metallic white were scraped on and white markel was stroked on.

Calico with gauze and wet gesso scraped in. Frayed threads were added. Fabric medium was scraped on and black ink was brushed on.

Fabric with scrim added.

Washed calico with gesso scraped on. Builder's scrim (a coarse, loose-weaved version of scrim) and tissue paper were added and scraped into the surface.

Washed calico with organic ink brushed in and lots of water added, plus gesso and builder's scrim at one edge.

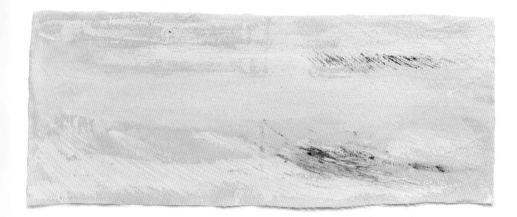

Washed calico with scraped gesso and acrylic colour added with the edge of a palette knife and pressed into the surface.

Unwashed calico with gesso scraped in, frayed threads and builder's scrim added to wet gesso and acrylic colour scraped into the surface.

Rubbings

Rubbings can be made with markel sticks or wax crayon. I have added ink on top.
I first cut some vessel shapes from thick card which I placed underneath a piece of paper or fabric. When held firmly, it is possible to make a rubbing from the card shape beneath.
I concentrated the colour at the edges of the shape and worked in a directional manner. I used light colour over dark paper and fabric for a strong contrast. Markel should be left to dry out or 'cure' for about twenty-four to forty-eight hours, after which it will be ready to work over or, in the case of fabric, stitching can be added.

Card templates for rubbings.

Rubbings with markel stick and a graphite pencil with ink over the top.

A rubbing made on fabric.

A rubbing on fabric with a card and a jug-shaped template using markel stick.

Abstraction

Some of Morandi's later works show the groups of objects simplified to the extent that they appear abstract. His watercolours show this particularly, with the image reduced to just a few simple blocks of soft colour and occasional lines. I decided to use just a few lines to indicate the vessel shapes and set these against bands and blocks of softly coloured shapes. If you work from successive drawings rather that always returning to look at the vessels themselves, it is easier to begin to simplify and leave out information. Also, if you work quickly, you can concentrate on just recording the essence and get the important marks down.

When drawing with line, it is helpful to be aware of the quality of the mark that you are making. If they are all the same weight and thickness, they can look dull and uninteresting. Try using different weights of felt pen from fine to very thick, or making the lines with a dip pen. Both these tools will give very different kinds of line. If you are drawing over a background that has been altered by adding scrim or gesso, the surface will be uneven, so your pen will not move across the surface easily, but you will get a line that has more character. If you want a very smooth, even line, use a smooth surface to draw on with a pen or pencil that will glide over it. Lines made with cut paper can give a very definite result, but can be a bit fiddly to stick down. This method is good for bold lines.

Pen and ink drawings reducing the image to just a few lines.

'It is an interesting exercise to see just how little information you need to show to be able to still read the image.'

Castings

To achieve some dimension, I have experimented with casting some shapes that were later added to either a drawing or to fabric.

I found a selection of tiny vessels and worked with plaster of Paris, paper pulp and metal mesh.

I used a material known as modroc, or plaster bandage, which is gauze impregnated with plaster of Paris. When wet, it is possible to mould it around a former. You need to work quickly as it sets in just a few minutes. It is also important to encase the former in cling film so that it is possible to remove the cast when hardened.

Paper pulp can be used in much the same way. Paint or scrape the pulp onto fine cotton or gauze and leave to set firm before removing from the former.

Fine metal mesh can be covered with fabric and joined with stitching by hand or machine. Use this material to form a shape over a vessel or bowl. Whether cut, bent, or folded, it will take the shape of the former.

A collection of small vessels, a clay bead and a piece of wood whittled to a vessel shape, all used for forming shapes.

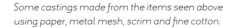

Some castings made from the items seen above using paper, metal mesh, scrim and fine cotton.

Colour studies

Morandi uses a neutral colour palette and I did some colour studies to establish the range of colours to use to interpret his work. The work is generally devoid of strong colour, so I needed to spend some time exploring neutrals and to work out just how to achieve them.

First of all I painted some sheets of paper using mixtures of black and white with small amounts of raw umber, cerulean blue, ultramarine, yellow ochre, lemon yellow and alizarin crimson. I used these papers to make some textures and to see what the effect would be when combining close tones together. These in turn suggested coloured marks for stitching.

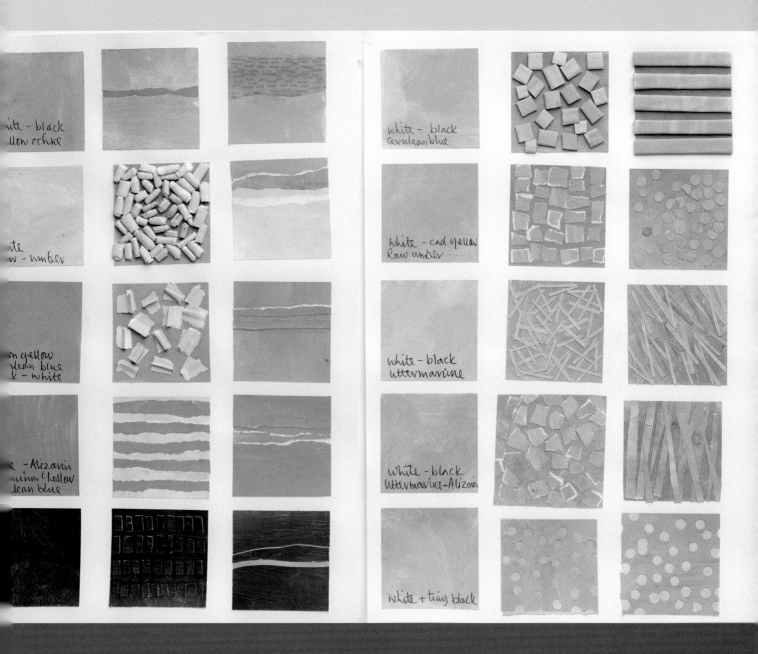

Developing ideas into stitch

I have used some of the stitches and techniques that can be found in traditional stumpwork, sometimes called raised work. This is embroidery with a three-dimensional effect, made using small wooden moulds or padded with cotton wool or similar. Separate pieces of fabric were made with stitching and applied over padding. I wanted the work to be small scale and finely worked. I have raised the still-life parts of the designs by using these methods. Backgrounds are stitched with directional straight stitching.

A stitch sampler developed from the colour studies on page 101, exploring colour relationships for backgrounds. Stitches include detached chain, blocks of satin stitch, cross hatching and directional straight stitch.

Exploring techniques

I have moved back and forth between drawing, collage and stitching
as the need has arisen. I found that I needed to refresh my memory
regarding shape, placement, colour and surface texture every so often.
This is especially necessary if working practice becomes fractured or
spasmodic. I have reused some of the techniques tried earlier, such as
the use of gesso and paint.

*A rubbing using markel sticks over card shapes, with
added hand stitch.*

*Detatched buttonhole stitch worked in a variety of threads onto a cotton
background with running stitch.*

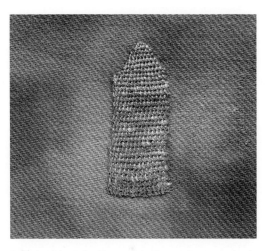

*Sample of detatched buttonhole. The stitch is worked with
the fabric framed so that tension can be controlled. Using
a variegated cotton thread, buttonhole stitch is worked
closely from side to side on the surface of the fabric. The
thread is anchored into the background fabric at the end
of each row of stitching. Use a blunt-ended needle so
that the thread is not pierced as the work proceeds.*

*Directional straight stitch on a linen
background, worked in a cotton thread of
similar weight throughout. By changing
the direction and colour of the stitching,
the small vessels are drawn.*

Using needlelace

Another technique used is a needlelace. This involves creating a small piece of fabric with a buttonhole stitch that can be applied to a background. It is made by first couching an outline of the shape with a double thread onto a smooth and shiny surface. I used a piece of Tyvek from an envelope. This stage (shown bottom left) is called a cordonnet.

The double thread should be carefully couched with small stitches about 3mm (⅛in) apart using an ordinary sewing thread. Begin couching at the folded end of the cordonnet thread and keep the two threads lying close together as you couch them around the shape. When you arrive back at your starting point, interlock the threads through the loop so that the lace does not fall apart when it is detatched from the support fabric. Finish the ends by turning them back on themselves in opposite directions and oversewing them to the laid threads. This completes the cordonnet. Detatched buttonhole is worked onto this framework on the surface of the support fabric to create a flat piece of fabric. There are many needlelace stitches and the techniques are explained in detail in some excellent books available on the subject, but I have only used straightforward buttonhole stitch to make the pieces for this book.

To begin stitching, attach the thread to the cordonnet by running it under several of the couching stitches and work a couple of buttonhole stitches firmly at this point. Continue by working buttonhole stitch into the spaces between the couching stitches across the shape. Link the working thread into the cordonnet and work back across the shape. Continue in this way until the shape is filled. The stitches may be close together or more widely spaced if a more open fabric is required. Either way, care should be taken with the tension of the stitching to keep it even, as it has a tendency to ride up. When complete, snip the couching stitches at the back of the support fabric to release the shape. One advantage of making small pieces in this way is that they may be manipulated to achieve some dimension by folding, curving or layering up as they are applied to a design.

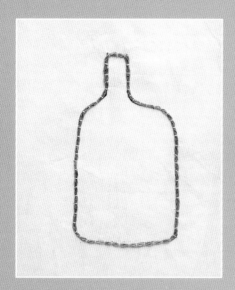

The cordonnet.

Detached buttonhole worked into the cordonnet to create a flat piece of fabric.

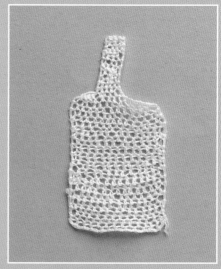

The finished needlelace fabric, released from the support.

Sample showing cast vessels on a markel rubbing with added stitching.

A small brooch constructed by making three tiny vessels from a thick thread oversewn with a fine one. It is possible to make these look different just by changing the thickness of the thread and the closeness of the oversewing. I worked them over my finger to support them while stitching. You could use a pencil or any other former of the right size and shape. I covered two strips of thick card with fabric and joined them together to make a shelf. The vessels were then stitched in place and a brooch pin attached to the back. It is easier to do this before any construction takes place.

Here, monoprinted fabric was torn into strips and applied to monoprinted paper. Small vessels are clustered together in the centre and I worked on top of these with detatched buttonhole and darning.

Here, the background was painted while the fabric was damp, allowing the colour to run. Rubbings were worked on top with pale-coloured markel sticks. I added straight stitches, open detached buttonhole and double Bruxelles stitch (where two stitches are worked into each loop).

Stitch sampler

I have made a small slip-case to hold samples of the stitches that I have used. Within the case is a fold-out sampler showing detatched buttonhole; a small dimensional vessel made by couching a machine cord; machine drawing; darning and machine texture made on a dissolvable support. Other samples show directional straight stitch and how to use straight stitch to achieve lines and breaks between areas of stitching.

The fold-out stitch sampler, shown opened out.

The slip case and the sampler shown folded.

Small Still Life: Vessels

A finished panel. Morandi sometimes divided his paintings into thirds. I have done this here by adding a piece of fine chiffon over the background fabric, which is cotton overlaid with scrim. I couched a thick thread to indicate where the vessels are standing. These were worked separately with a variety of threads oversewn to join them together. The foreground was worked with directional straight stitching with a silk thread. The top and bottom areas of dense stitching serve to encase the vessels in a kind of frame, reflecting the way Morandi compressesd his vessels into a central area.

Further development

A piece of stitching developed from the abstracted drawings shown on page 99. I have made the bold lines with a black thread and worked them with small straight stitches to form a line. The background is worked with directional straight stitching.

John Piper (1903–1992) was a prolific artist working throughout the greater part of the twentieth century, exploring abstraction, architecture, landscape, printmaking, stained glass window and tapestry design and collage. He was a war artist during World War II, and he was involved with the 'Recording Britain' project that aimed to preserve a record of buildings which might be destroyed by bombing. He was also an author and critic.

He was committed to continuing experimentation in all media, especially printmaking. His early work as a painter was inspired by Picasso, Braque and Matisse, and he embraced modernism and abstraction through the influence of Mondrian, Ben Nicholson and Paul Nash. His abstract work was concerned with coastal subjects, showing flotsam from the beach, natural erosion and weather, geology in the form of rocks and cliffs and architectural details of harbours, boats and marine symbols. These subjects were illustrated using collage, watercolour and inks.

Piper saw abstract art as an expression of a calm order beneath the chaos and conflict of the time, since it was devoid of all decoration and detail, sentimentality and purpose.

However, Piper later became disillusioned with abstraction and reverted to naturalistic subjects such as seascapes. He returned to the architectural, topographical and historical subjects which were his true interests. In this he was inspired by Frederick Cotman, JMW Turner, William Blake and Samuel Palmer. He wrote of Cotman's work, 'These drawings dwell on three facts: the beauty of the texture of decaying stonework and woodwork; the clear light of East Anglia; and the wholeness, the oneness of each church in relation to its landscape.' He felt strongly that art had to develop according to the 'influences one truly experiences, within oneself.' His called his interest in place, 'the basic and unexplainable thing about my painting'.

Besides painting, John Piper explored collage, using a mixture of string, doilies, marbled paper and scrim. He was also a writer, art critic and magazine editor. His subject was the English countryside and the architecture within it. This led to the editing and writing of the Shell Guides, guide books to English counties, in collaboration with the poet, John Betjeman. His painting at this time depicted old buildings, churches, and details of the ordinary object. He was drawn to the 'attractively untidy' industrial scenery in a state of decay, which he found to have aesthetic beauty. He was fascinated by the diaologue between past and present that John Ruskin described as, '...that agedness in the midst of active life which binds the old and new into harmony'.

John Piper's interest in the landscape of Great Britain resonates with mine. The places he visited are those that have inspired me and his printed images of old churches and buildings strike a chord that is hard to dismiss. I have therefore chosen to look at these rather than the early abstractions or his war work.

Where to see the work

The Imperial War Museum, Tate Britain and Morley College, London; the Herbert Art Gallery, Coventry; tapestries in Chichester and Hereford Cathedrals, Museum of Reading, Berkshire. Stained glass windows can be seen in many churches around Britain including Coventry Cathedral and Robinson College, Cambridge.

My painting from one of John Piper's works, 'Binham Abbey, 1981'.

Reasons for choosing John Piper

Many years ago I found the book *Piper's Places* on the shelf in my local library. The images I discovered within it were captivating and I borrowed the book many times before I acquired a copy of my own. I love the loose, scribbly style of mark-making in Piper's work, the printed textures and his theatrical use of colour. I am drawn to the places that he illustrated too, many of which are particular favourites that I visit when time allows. So when considering which artists to choose for this book, John Piper was an obvious choice. I decided to explore monoprint with my drawings of buildings in some of the places that John Piper has recorded, namely Malmesbury in Wiltshire; Cornwall; and Pembrokeshire in Wales.

'The sea is the mystery that lies beyond the flat fields and the woods and downs, the rough moors and the Black country recesses: never far away.'

John Piper

Inspiration and development

Inspired by John Piper's idea of the aesthetic beauty of 'pleasing decay', I began by making some drawings of buildings. I chose Malmesbury Cathedral, as it has a ruined area next to the main building which is overgrown with trees and bushes. I felt that what I could see was in the spirit of John Piper's prints and would give me the right kind of imagery with which to experiment. I took photographs to use when back in the studio, but also made drawings at the site. I have used pen and ink washes, charcoal and collage to really get to know the subject before moving onto the next stage.

I decided to use monoprint to interpret John Piper's images, many of which are printed. This technique gives me the opportunity to experiment with my drawings by printing onto tissue paper and layering with colour.

Malmesbury Cathedral – charcoal and white chalk.

'The stonework is crumbling and there are vistas of archways, remnants of pillars and patterns in the tracery around doorways.'

Malmesbury Cathedral – pencil, ink and watercolour.

Malmesbury Cathedral – pen, ink and wash.

Detail of stone carving – graphite, watercolour and chalk.

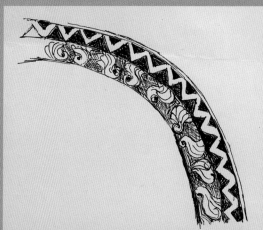

Malmesbury Cathedral – pen, ink and wash.

Design and development

There are so many ways to explore monoprint. Simply inking up a plate with colour and taking a print from it can give some lovely textures, depending on the amount and consistency of ink on the plate. It is possible to draw into the ink or to take some of it away by wiping or scraping. Mark-making with a variety of tools provides many effects to inspire stitching, as does working with resists; while drawing into the back of the paper is ideal for line work. All these methods work well on fabric too, so whatever is done at the design stage can also be done with fabric – with one exception: the tearing of paper. Fabric will only usually tear in the direction of the grain unless it has begun to disintegrate, when it becomes soft enough to pull apart. The torn edge of paper, with its characteristic soft broken edge and meandering line, is hard to replicate in fabric.

A monoprint showing ink scraped away from the inked plate, with coloured tissue paper added.

A print taken from an inked plate. A square of coloured tissue is added.

To add detail to a basic monoprint, place a sheet of thin paper over an inked plate and draw an image or make linear marks using a pencil or ballpoint pen on the back of the paper. These marks will print much more strongly than the rest of the print as more pressure has been applied to the paper.

For a resist, ink a plate with the desired colour, then add a shape cut or torn from thin paper over the ink. When paper is placed over the plate, only the inked area will print. The paper resist can be used later as a collaged image on a design. Very detailed images can be created with this method if a scalpel is used to cut the paper resist, but softer edges may be achieved by tearing paper, which is largely what I have done with my designs.

Folded book of ideas

I have cut, torn and pieced papers together and made a folded book full of ideas to take into fabric and thread. The folded book form is a convenient way to store designs, as the pieces take up less space than they would in a portfolio and can sit next to sketchbooks in your bookcase.

I started with an A1 size sheet of good quality cartridge paper and began to make splashes of colour by tearing pieces of red and yellow tissue paper and randomly pasting them down. I also made some prints directly onto the paper using a screenprint of a quote by the artist, Grayson Perry. The placing of these prints was random too, sometimes overlapping the tissue paper. Then I stuck down some monoprints, made on tissue paper with black ink. I tore them up and filled spaces with them, overlapping them here and there, trying not to get 'precious' with the imagery. Tissue paper can be difficult to glue to another surface. I find it easier to put the glue onto the firmer cartridge paper, then drop the tissue paper onto this, preventing the tissue paper from becoming too wet and fragile to work with.

The reason for choosing to make monoprints on tissue paper is that it is difficult to get a good print from cartridge paper as it is sometimes too thick, especially when drawing on the back of the paper. Also, I knew that I intended to fold the paper into a book, so I did not want too much bulk. Tissue paper is also transparent when stuck down so that where it overlaps colour or other detail, it allows this to show through.

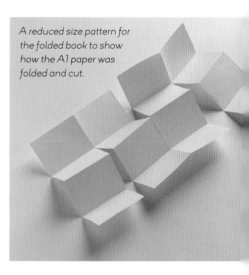

A reduced size pattern for the folded book to show how the A1 paper was folded and cut.

I left the paper to dry before dividing it into four sections in both directions. I folded it in half and in half again in landscape format and also in the portrait direction. I opened out the paper and cut along the first folded line as far as the last section, then along the last fold line as far as the last section. I then turned the paper round and cut from the opposite side, through the middle fold as far as the last section (see right). I folded the paper sections back and forth until I got a compact book form with the imagery to the outside. I opened out the pages to reveal several compositions that had been arrived at randomly (see opposite).

Further developments

It is possible to further develop the pages of the book by adding or over-pasting tissue monoprints or colour. You can also add lines by drawing into the imagery. I have used a reed pen with ink to add architectural details. A further development would be to cover both sides of the paper with colour and print before cutting and folding.

I have worked with monoprints and responded to ideas from the folded book designs using piecing, patching, cutting, tearing and drawing on top.

'I wanted to try and capture the loose style of John Piper's work with imagery of buildings, abstraction and random use of colour.'

A design that is the basis of the finished panel on pages 126–7. I made a collage with various monoprints and combined them to suggest architectural details.

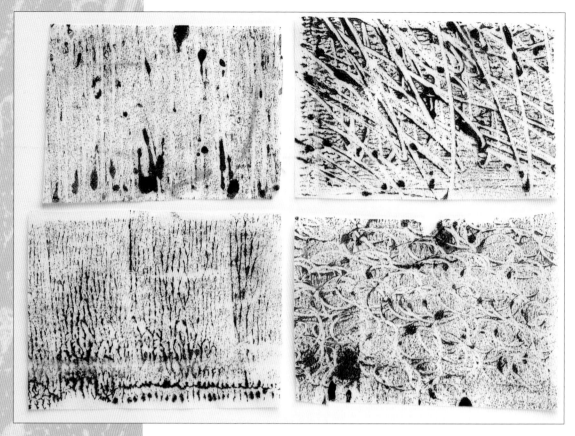

Four different textures printed onto fusible web. Marks are made into the inked plate with a variety of tools, a stick, a fine paint scraper and a brush.

Printing on fabric

I made prints onto a variety of fabrics including very fine transparent fabric so that I could use it in the same way as I have used tissue paper at the design stage. I also printed onto fusible web, as this can be ironed onto a print or over stitching to blend or add a subtle texture.

Monoprint on sheer fabrics can be applied over stronger prints to give soft effects. From left to right: silk chiffon, very fine muslin, silk chiffon.

Monoprinted cotton fabric. Left: yellow ink was printed first ,then overprinted with black. I scribbled into the inked plate first. A second print was taken with the same process in red.

A print was taken with red ink and overlaid with a further print in black. I drew into the back of the fabric with a ballpoint pen to make the lines, taking care not to press the fabric too heavily, as I did not want to transfer too much ink in other areas.

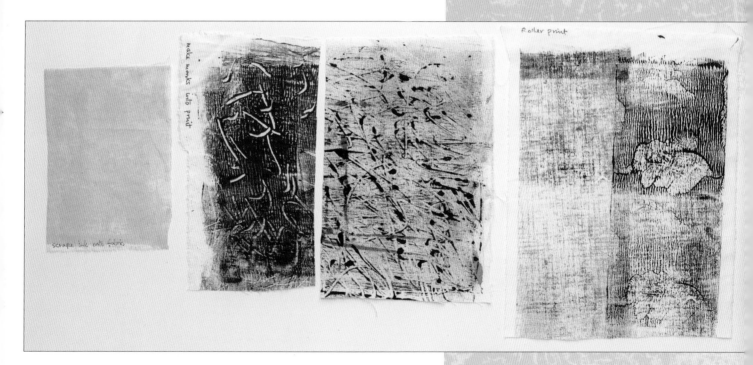

Further monoprints, from left to right: yellow ink scraped onto fabric; marks made into red ink prior to printing; layers of colour from several prints, the final layer in black with a scribble mark made into the inked plate; and finally, ink applied to the fabric with a roller.

Stitching on a dissolvable background

Working with stitch textures made on a dissolvable background gives me a fabric that is open and transparent once the background is washed away after stitching. This can be used to overlay onto prints or for colour diffusing and softening effects. I have made some scribbly marks with the sewing machine using free machine stitching to create the effect of drawing. Adding these marks at a separate stage rather than working directly onto the printed fabric gives a different look to the work and avoids the problem of distortion and puckering of the fabric. I don't particularly like working with an embroidery hoop so this is avoided too.

I have combined the free machine stitching with couching by hand using a variety of thicknesses of thread: fine and bold, including a narrow tape for a stronger line. These marks can be close together or spaced out, and they can be made in any direction or used to emphasise areas within the image.

Making fabrics on a wire frame is a useful technique too as it can be cut and pieced, or applied as a shape. It can be as open or as dense as you wish, applied by hand or machine, or bonded to the surface.

I have limited the colour of the stitching, working almost exclusively with black thread, whether by hand or machine. When I am making fabric, I use a device that enables me to work with thread on a large cone, which is economical when using a quantity of the same colour – in this case black. It is a strong structure that holds the thread in place at the back of the machine and can hold any cone that is not suitable to be attached to the machine in the usual manner (see right).

The techniques that I have chosen have given me a flexible palette with which to interpret my designs. The use of simple running stitch provides a mark that can link areas together or move a colour around a design as a final embellishment where needed.

Far left: My device for working with a large cone of thread that will not fit into a sewing machine.

Couching and free machine stitching are added to monoprinted fabric, with additions of fine silk organdie.

When the machine stitching was complete, I washed the dissolvable support away, first cutting away any surplus fabric. I then pinned the result out onto a piece of polystyrene. This ensures that the work remains stretched to the correct size and shape and avoids distortion. Use hot or cold water depending on the type of support used. Sometimes you need to wash it several times before all the sticky residue has gone.

Monoprinted fabrics are pieced and patched together to form this design. An arch shape is cut from fabric made by machine using the dissolvable support method. This is hand stitched to the design. Further stitching by hand is added to blend areas together and provide detail.

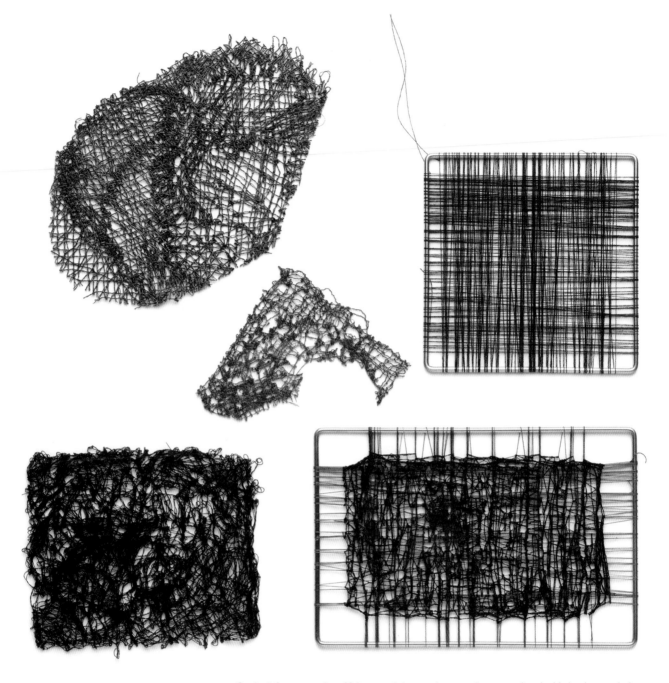

On the left are samples of fabric made by machine stitching on a dissolvable background, showing a variety of the marks and density that can be achieved. On the right are wire frames wound with a machine thread. The one at the bottom has machine stitch added ready for cutting off the frame.

Making fabric on a frame

This is the method I use. Tie the thread to the frame and then wind the thread onto the frame until there is enough density. The frame can be wound in the opposite direction if you wish to create a denser fabric. Winding in one direction only will give a more linear fabric, with the threads drawing together as stitching proceeds. Crossing them with a second winding stabilises the movement of the wound thread to an extent. However, there will still be some movement that can be controlled with careful stitching.

A sample showing the use of a patterned fabric made by the machine method on a dissolvable support. Fabrics can be made to an exact size and pattern if required.

Architectural Panel

Working from the design on pages 118-119, I have cut and pieced this panel from a collection of prints. These are blended together with directional stitching and couching, using a variety of thicknesses of thread, responding to marks in the printed fabric. I have laid a cotton tape to outline and emphasise the shape of the windows, sills or doorways. Some small areas are embellished with detached chain stitch and running stitch is used to soften the coloured areas and take the colour into adjoining areas of the design.

Henri Matisse (1869–1954) is one of the twentieth century's most loved and respected artists. He was a prolific practitioner and his work is widely distributed around the world.

Matisse began his life in French Flanders in a town known for its woollen mills, lace and luxury fabrics. When he was twenty-one, he left for Paris, where he trained to become a painter. He later moved to the South of France, where he spent the greater part of his life in Nice, inspired by the bright, clear light of the Mediterranean.

Matisse came from a long line of weavers, so it is not surprising that textiles were in his blood. He collected textiles from the time he was a student until the last years of his life, and referred to his collection as 'my working library'. He amassed such treasures as Persian carpets, Arab embroideries, African wall hangings, cushions, curtains, costumes and patterned screens and backcloths, which served as inspiration for his painting. He would take fabrics with him when he travelled so that he could continue to work on them. He was skilled at using scissors to cut and piece. There are reports of people watching him 'drawing with scissors'. He used fabrics to compose his pictures, cutting and placing coloured paper shapes on his canvases with pins.

He enjoyed the immediacy and spontaneity of this design process, which was the result of being exposed to the experimental practices of the weavers during his childhood. These weavers used hand looms to create individual one-off pieces of luxury cloth that had a fluidity and a visual sophistication not achievable via mechanised methods.

Whilst a student at the Ecole des Beaux-Arts in Paris, Matisse was frustrated with the sterility of the teaching methods, and surrounded himself with an inspirational collection of fabrics with strong colours and textures. Fabrics were to be not only a practical resource throughout his life but an inspirational one too, becoming an integral component of his still life paintings and as a backdrop to the figurative compositions.

He was a founder artist of the Fauves movement in 1900, together with André Derain, and Picasso was a life-long friend. Cézanne was influential in Matisse's use of the decorative in that it allowed him to see Cézanne's view of the world through fresh eyes. He mixed actual items with the same objects depicted on cloth within a composition so that the real was integrated with the decorative. The motifs were often painted as flat shapes, whether real or imagined, with foregrounds inter-related with backgrounds.

The seven months that Matisse spent in Morocco inspired compositions of figures set within interiors, showing flat decorative pattern in the backgrounds and figures dressed in eastern costume.

During World War II, Matisse began to develop his cutouts. He put painting aside, preferring to work directly with coloured paper shapes. In 1947 he produced a book of cutouts entitled 'Jazz'. Towards the end of his life, he experienced ill health and was confined to a wheelchair, but he continued to work with cut paper and designed a stained glass window for the Chapel of the Rosary at Vence. He died in Nice, aged 84.

I am inspired by the colour, marks and treatments of surface in Matisse's work, in particular the still life paintings. I like the decorative quality of his work and, while reading about his life, I learned about the importance of textiles as inspiration. It interests me that early experience can have such a strong effect on future work, and that reflecting on one's early experiences makes sense of decisions subsequently taken. The textile connection provides a way into understanding the work of a popular and highly commended artist.

Where to see the work

Matisse was a prolific and popular artist, whose work has been collected around the world. Many pieces are in private collections, but the following are a few of the museums that have some of his work: The Baltimore Museum of Art, Maryland; The Victoria & Albert Museum, London;
The National Gallery, London;
The Metropolitan Museum of Art, New York; The Pushkin State Museum of Fine Arts, Moscow; Musée de l'Orangerie, Paris.

Opposite

My interpretation of Matisse's 'Purple Robe and Anemones', 1937.

Working from the inspiration

I have combined the still life subject with the decorative aspect of fabrics and explored pattern and shape in combination with composite stitching. I wanted to create highly decorative pieces using what could develop into wall hangings or textiles for interiors, such as cushions, curtains or possibly rugs.

I began by collecting together images of textiles and still life objects and arranging them together. I took photographs of these and made simple line drawings from photographic prints. This produced images that were flattened, excluding spatial considerations of perspective, and this made them more decorative. Stylised shapes were repeated to build pattern, following Matisse's example.

An arrangement of patterned cloth with an image of a stitched vessel added.

A pen and wash sketch made from the arrangement.

An arrangement of patterned cloth with still–life objects.

A pen sketch of the arrangement.

Drawings made from Matisse's paintings to show background patterns.

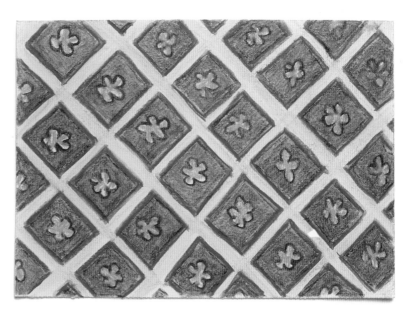

Design and development

I made collages from the drawings using painted papers; cutting and piecing the composition. Simplified, stylised shapes were freely cut using scissors, without prior drawing, and moved around until I was happy with the arrangement. The coloured papers that I used were randomly painted with acrylics. They were patchy and textured in some areas so when they were cut up, there was some irregularity in colour and surface.

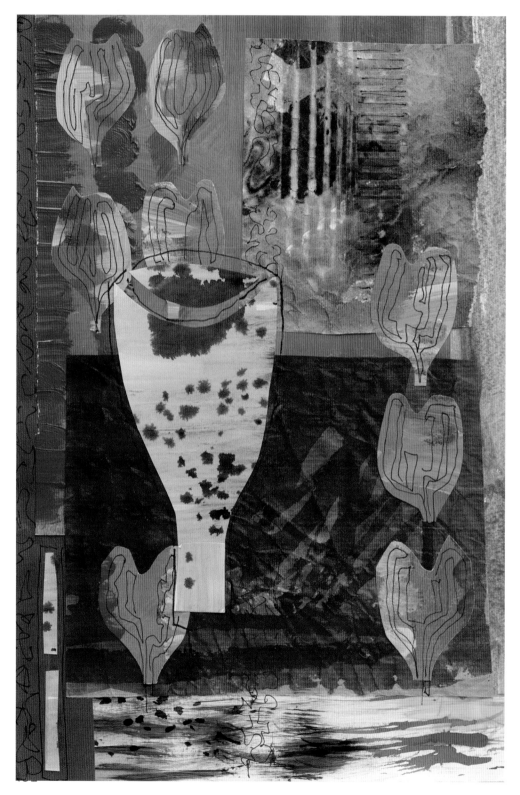

These two collages were made using the drawings from pages 130–131.

I also explored making designs using old photographs, again, cutting and piecing randomly to create pattern.

Many of Matisse's paintings of interiors show patterned backgrounds. I recorded some of these as they give suggestions for stitch and show that complicated decorative fabrics can be simplified down to just a few lines and shapes.

Old photographs were cut up and rearranged with a drawing of a still-life object added.

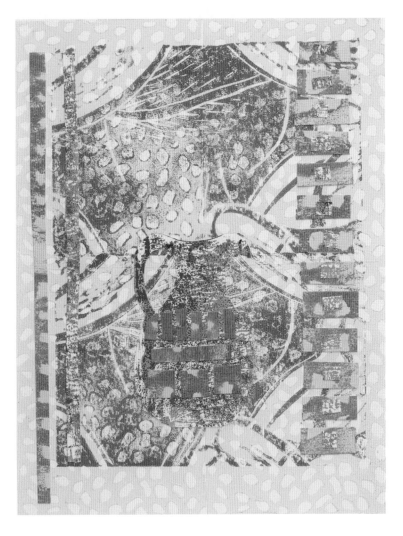

Here I have created a collage using papers that I had printed, to explore pattern on pattern.

Further processes

I was anxious to find my own method of combining still life imagery with the decorative aspect of patterned fabric, and eventually decided to work with digital print. There are a growing number of companies offering to print original designs onto cloth. I decided to try this method of transferring a design, so had my collaged designs and stitched samples printed onto cotton fabric. I was able to enlarge them too, enabling me to scale up the stitching. It is also possible to have the images repeat printed. This would be a useful process if quilting were to be the eventual outcome.

I selected one of the enlarged designs and pieced several smaller stitched pieces onto it. Further stitching was needed to integrate the individual elements into a resolved image.

A digital print made from the collage on page 132.

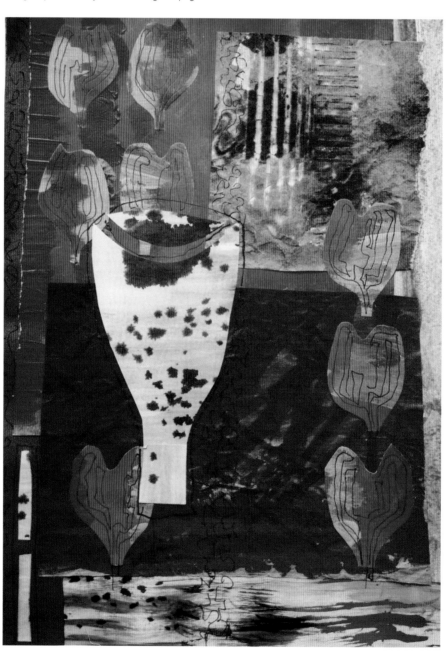

Composition

The placing of elements within a design or picture to create a unified and balanced image is the process of composition. When the building blocks of composition are examined and understood, a greater sense of appreciation of painting can be achieved and it is well worth practising this.

Placing similar units together or in a sequence will produce repeat pattern and can give a pleasing harmony to the work. Disharmony may be deliberately used to create a discordant image by misplacing some of these units.

Symmetry appeals to our sense of order, but be wary of making a design that is predictable or boring. An asymmetrical design is often more dynamic and pleasing.

Key shapes should not be placed dead centre, and placing them too high up will give a feeling of instability, while putting them too near the bottom may look as if they are falling out of the picture frame. Dividing your image into thirds horizontally and vertically is a good rule of thumb, and placing your focal point or key shape at an intersection will look balanced.

All elements of a picture compete for attention so the most important area should stand out, with all other elements such as shape, texture, colour or line having a supporting role.

The viewer's eye should be led around the image, so space between shapes should allow this to happen. I often see designs where the individual components are too widely spaced, which gives a disjointed image that is hard to read.

The rhythm of a piece will rely on some degree of contrast, whether that be in colour, texture or scale. A dark shape will appear heavier than a light one of the same size, and red and yellow are both highly visible, so that the eye is drawn to them.

Scale and proportion both relate to size. Scale is how large something is and proportion is how much of it there is in relation to its surroundings.

So there is a lot to consider when putting a design together. If you are aware of what to look out for, you can make creative judgments from the point of knowledge instead of hoping for the best and relying too heavily on intuition.

I have divided the picture space into sections. The jug stands firmly in the bottom section, but makes contact with all other areas, linking the composition together. When stitched, the jug could be the brightest or most textural area, creating a strong focal point.

Experiments with composition

I began by making thumbnail sketches to get a feel for what kind of image I wanted. When exploring ideas, I find it a valuable process to just put down anything that pops into my head without trying too hard to evaluate the information. I have divided the picture space into a variety of shapes and placed the principal shape within these. Some work well and some do not but it is a method of recording ideas in a short space of time. When you see them set out on the sketchbook page, you can soon see which are the best and which are worth taking on into fabric and thread.

The samples shown here and on page 135 have been put together using a mixture of my own hand-coloured paper, magazine papers and decorative paper bags that I have collected over time. The shapes are randomly cut out with scissors and placed according to the rules of composition, with consideration given to colour, balance, scale and proportion and some reference to my initial sketches.

The same process can be applied to cutting and piecing with patterned fabric. The sample above, right uses fabrics from my collection. The background is a piece of fabric given to me when teaching in Sweden, and the others are remnants from garments that I have altered. It appeals to me that fabric can hold such memories of people and events and can be worked into new pieces of textile art that can tell a personal story, besides being appreciated by others who may not know the significance.

Stitch samplers

My aim for the stitched pieces inspired
by Matisse was to achieve a highly decorative
surface and to display the richness that intensively
worked stitching has.

I have worked with a family of stitches known as composite
stitches. The structure of these stitches relies on a foundation that
is laid down first before completing the second stage of the stitch.
The stitches used are raised chain band, raised stem, lock stitch, wave
stitch, whipped and laced running and laced herringbone, supported by
other useful additions such as backstitch, couching, running stitch
and detached chain.

The examples shown opposite show a range of possibilities. The
stitches look different when a variety of types of thread are used:
matt, shiny, smooth or woolly. I have used perle cotton, silk threads,
crochet cotton, wool and linen. The direction can be varied
too and I have arranged the stitching to show a series of
circles that serves to link the separate samples. All
these stitches may be found in books that are
dedicated to showing how to work
them, or online.

Laced herringbone worked in lines and shapes.

Lock stitch and wave stitch shown as line and filling shapes.

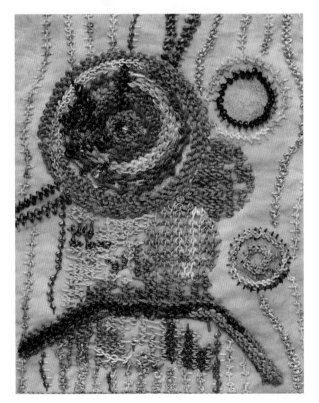

Raised chain band, showing lines, filling a shape, padded with thread and worked randomly.

Raised stem band showing the stitch used as lines, filling a shape, and padded with felt. The background is worked with a simple straight stitch.

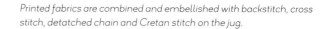

Printed fabrics are combined and embellished with backstitch, cross stitch, detatched chain and Cretan stitch on the jug.

Printed fabrics are combined and composite stitching added: raised chain band for the central jug, wave stitch for the background and laced herringbone and raised chain band for the borders.

A printed pattern is embellished with couching, backstitch and darning. The jug is stitched with detached chain stitch.

Patterns are created by combining small straight stitches, and some raised chain band is worked onto some of these. The vessels are made from 'minced' fabric. Buttonhole stitch is worked into the foreground.

A section of the border with couched silk fabric strips and darning in the central squares.

A section of a digital print is embellished with lock stitch and raised chain band for the borders.

Printed, patterned fabric shapes with added stitching: raised chain band on the central vessel, couching on the small yellow shapes, lock stitch on the right-hand border, laced herringbone at the bottom and whipped straight stitches on the left. The background is detached chain.

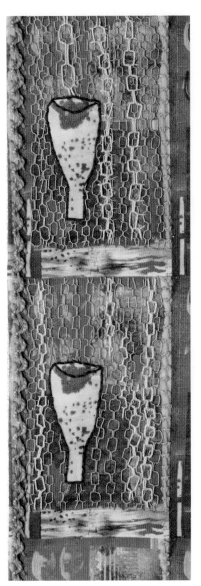

141

Wall Hangings

I have combined one of my enlarged digital prints with some stitched pieces and worked additional stitching to blend these together to make a coherent whole composition. This enabled me to create a much larger piece and to block out some of the parts of the background that were not working very well. I needed to consider the balance of all the component parts, how the colour worked as a whole and where the focal point was to be.

A small piece of digitally printed fabric was used to make this brooch. Raised chain band highlights the vessel, with straight stitching around the border.

A repeat pattern was digitally printed from one of my collages. I then added a previously stitched piece to it and blended it to the background by adding further stitching.

Index

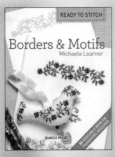

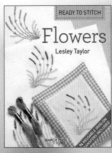

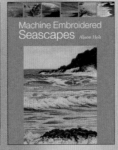

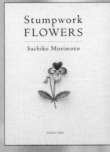

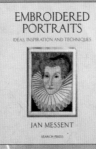

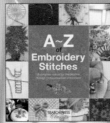